DEATH NEEDS ANSWERS

The Cold-Blooded Murder of Dr. John Yelenic

Andrea Niapas

Copyright © 2013 by Andrea Niapas. All rights reserved.

All rights reserved. No part of this book may be used or reproduced in any manner whatsoever without written permission except in the case of brief quotations embodied in critical articles or reviews.

ISBN: 978-935591-13-9

First printing, April 2013

This edition was printed by Grelin Press
P.O. Box 367, New Kensington, PA 15068
(724) 334-8240   grelinpress@aol.com

This book is dedicated to all victims and
co-victims of homicides.

*Let the flames of fear
be fueled by justice.*

TABLE OF CONTENTS

Acknowledgements 7
Introduction 9

Two's a Pair . . . Three's a Crowd
Chapter 1 15
Chapter 2 25
Chapter 3 31
Chapter 4 37
Chapter 5 43
Chapter 6 53

Through the Kitchen Door
Chapter 7 63
Chapter 8 69
Chapter 9 75

Death Needs Answers
Chapter 10 87
Chapter 11 97

Ides of March
Chapter 12 103
Chapter 13 123
Chapter 14: The Blairsville Slaying and the
    Dawn of DNA Computing by
    Dr. Mark Perlin 129

Timeline 149
Author's Documented Investigation 2008-2010 155
Where Are They Now? 169

Author's Final Thoughts 171
Photo Gallery 177

APPENDIX

Entries Leading up to Divorce 189
Marital Agreement 191
Crime Report 207
Crime Scene Log 208
Report by Officer Jill Gaston 211
Death Certificate 212
Police Interview with Dennis Vaughn 213
Grand Jury Report 215
Press Release: Arrest of Kevin Foley 229
Impact Statements 234
PSTA Statement: Sentencing of Kevin Foley 246
PA Code on Murder 247
Glossary 251

About the Author 253

ACKNOWLEDGEMENTS

To ALL those who took their time to provide me with interviews over the phone and on film which helped me better understand Dr. John Yelenic. Also to those who declined my invitation which only kept me investigating. The opportunity and encouragement Mary Ann Clark extended to me throughout the years while developing the documentary and this book. To my husband Gus who listened, directed, and re-directed me during the writings and re-writes. Nicolina Lanni at Cineflix Inc. for following through on her commitment to present Dr. John Yelenic's story on television. All the local media reporters who kept the homicide investigation front page and at the top of the news broadcast for days, weeks, months, and years. To the many readers and re-readers of the manuscript as it was going through transitions. Pat Childs who widened my eyes. Most of all to the dedicated friends Tim Abbey, Dennis Vaughn, Margaret McCartin, Roberta Mack and Dr. Maria Tacelosky, who took friendship and loyalty to the highest level any friend could have. And, a special thanks to Dr. Mark Perlin and his Cybergenetics staff, especially Kiersten Dormer and Jennifer Hornyak, for all their assistance every step of the way.

INTRODUCTION

Let me take you back to the dawn of a new year: *January 2007, when I began investigating.*

On a cold snowy morning after two cups of coffee I turned and glanced through the newspaper that had just arrived. I invariably begin with the local section. Always wanting to know what is going on close to home, I guess. On this particular morning one headline caught my eye titled, "They're Frustrated by Tight-Lipped Police," reported by Richard Gazarik of the Westmoreland *Tribune-Review*.

It was a follow up story about the murder of a dentist in Blairsville by the name of Dr. John Yelenic back in April 2006. In the article it was stated that friends of the slain dentist were seeking media exposure to sustain the case in the public eye. Usually at that point most are aware and fear the police investigations will evolve into a cold case.

The interviews were given by Mary Ann Clark (cousin of the victim, Dr. Yelenic) and his two college friends, Tim Abbey and Dennis Vaughn. They expressed their disappointment with the local police efforts for not apprehending the murderer/murderers to date. As I read further into the article, their statements attracted me in like a piece of metal sliding straight into a magnetic field. I just had to do something right then and there. So I did what I do best . . .made the phone call!

Grabbing a phone book, I found the listing for the Reilly and Yelenic Dental Practice located on Market Street in Blairsville and began dialing the numbers. A receptionist answered directing me to speak with Mary Ann Clark, then began to rattle off her home phone number as I jotted it down quickly. There was no turning back as the phone began to ring. I was committed!

After the third ring I thought the answering machine was ready to kick in. To my surprise a female voice answered identifying herself as Mary Ann Clark.

Going into a call I never quite know how it will turn out, so I listen very closely to the tone of the voice on the other end of the line. It alerts me as to where in the "cycle of closure" that person is fixated. The range can be from reacting as if it just happened yesterday to circumventing to downright anger. The tone of this voice was strong, loud, precise, and quick. I knew it was from a person who wanted to hear something important from the caller or at least something to assist with the investigation underway in the murder of her cousin.

Mary Ann calmly listened to me explain why I was calling. Stating that I had been aware of the case but had not read any updates for months until December 28, 2006, and I was stunned that it was still unsolved. She explained that it was her understanding that the police had not come up with any leads. She went on to express that everyone among family, friends, and associates are so angry at this point that they are afraid John's death will slip between the cracks.

I never like to hear that conclusion from co-victims. Nine chances out of ten, those closest to the victim can see that coming way before the rest of us. At that moment it was time to jump in. I stated that I produce documentaries through research and that I would like to assemble a testimonial film honoring Dr. John Yelenic's life. It would consist of photos of John growing up, and interviews by his family, friends, patients, teachers and so forth. I also mentioned that perhaps by developing this tool it would give everyone closest to him an opportunity to express their heartfelt memories. This project will hopefully help ease their grief in a positive constructive fashion. A DVD format is used so copies will be available for everyone. This would be done pro bono for the family. I asked her to just think about it and if she was interested to give me a call back. After giving her my number, she thanked me and we hung up.

Usually I just step back at that point and let destiny take over. If it is to be, it will be. That call took place on Tuesday, January 2, 2007. By Thursday, January 4th, Clark called me back eagerly wanting to go forward as soon as possible with the procedure. She had arranged for a group of John's friends (who extended their Christmas vacations in the area for this meeting to take place), along with neighbors and relatives, to gather at Clark Metal (her husband's business facility) to begin taping on Friday, January 5, 2007 at 1:00 p.m.

The interviewing process went on for several years. Yes, years because the Dr. John Yelenic homicide investigation got caught up in a nightmare. I documented hours upon hours of film footage pertaining to individuals involved with John, Michele Magyar-

Kamler-Yelenic, and Kevin Foley. As well as uncovering motives, opportunities, means, and evidence. This has been an ongoing investigation since April 13, 2006 and will continue until those persons *accountable* for the murder of Dr. John Yelenic are brought to justice.

For me what started out to be a thirty to forty-five minute DVD testimonial turned out to become a case study in unsuccessful parent-child relationships that influenced the tragedies of three generations to date. Not to mention a murder, incarceration, and the jury is still out on any future fallout.

While researching the murder case of John Yelenic—a young, handsome, admired, prominent dentist who was murdered in Blairsville, Pennsylvania back in 2006—I became aware that two other characters were intertwined. They were his estranged (soon to be ex-wife) Michele Magyar-Kamler-Yelenic and her live-in boyfriend, Pennsylvania State Trooper Kevin Foley. All three of these individuals appeared to possess unique personality traits. When I began to dig deeper into how they acquired these traits, I was lured right back to the relationship they had with their parent/parents.

So why and how did these unique individuals come together? What purpose did it serve? What good came out of all the human cartilage left behind? The old proverb states that "*The son pays for the sins of the father.*" Only in this case, the twist is at the mercy of Michele Magyar-Kamler-Yelenic. She's presently playing single parent to her adoptive sons (in every sense of the word adoptive, sharing no DNA). The son she and John Yelenic adopted is known as JJ (John Jay Yelenic), and will turn into a "Golden Goose" at age eighteen when he is set to inherit a 1.7 million dollar life insurance policy left to him by his father.

Mary Ann Clark had also introduced a civil case (May 2008) against Trooper Kevin Foley, Michele Yelenic and several of the troopers of the Indiana State Police Barracks, including the commander. The basis for the suit is their negligence in preventing the murder of Dr. John Yelenic.

The above action could materialize after Kevin Foley has exhausted all his appeals in the Pennsylvania court system. As of January 4, 2012, his final appeal at the Superior Court level has been denied. Will he try to appeal to the Supreme Court of Pennsylvania? Any prisoner incarcerated for life has just one goal in mind . . . to GET OUT! Felons have all the time in the world to study their trial transcripts as well as laws of their state. There are appeal attorneys willing to take on the challenge of finding a loophole in the trial testimony and calling for a retrial. Reasonable doubt is what they strive to seek from a new jury.

CHAPTER ONE

Taught to feel good about ourselves is essential in our quest to love one another.

Death Needs Answers . . .

In the murder of Dr. John Yelenic I examine how three lives came together through fate or circumstances (you be the judge) and resulted in a horrible senseless homicide. Are there winners or losers in a murder? Perhaps the ones that get away with it think they have won, but in truth do they? Or are they just tricking themselves into believing their own form of reality?

To completely understand this murder mystery, we must go way back to where the story began. I'll start with the one whose death should have never happened: John Yelenic. He died way before his time . . . or was he cursed? I reviewed hundreds of photos of John from the Yelenic's family albums. Every time I looked deep into his eyes I saw sadness. The whole soul of this person was lost, not to anger nor to revenge, but in an endless searching to make strangers his friends. He was taught the Golden Rule as a child and abided by it. Photos of happier times showed him smiling. To the onlooker, however, it appeared the smiles needed to be taken at face value. What was he searching for? They say be careful for what you wish for. But at the time do we even realize that we are in a predicament? Whatever the situation, one usually just tries to do the best he or she can do.

 John was raised to ask for little. Even later in life when he became financially successful, his friends say he still remained a humble man. John was always there—for anyone at anytime—offering what he could through emotional support or financial assistance. Maggie, a long time friend of his, called him the "glue" that held all his friends together throughout the years. It appeared that the supportive nurturing John received as a young child definitely made him into a man of substance.

 John Joseph Yelenic, Jr. was born February 20, 1967, in Blairsville, Pennsylvania, to Mary Lois and John Joseph Yelenic, Sr. In just three short months, John Jr.'s life was changed forever. One cold and rainy Sunday afternoon around 2:00 p.m., Mary Lois placed her son in his crib for a nap. Walking into the kitchen, she began to prepare lunch for her husband who was due back home momentarily from a business meeting in Monroeville. The phone rang. A man identified himself as a police officer and asked her if she was Mrs. John J. Yelenic residing at 452 South Spring Street Blairsville. By now her intuition must have kicked in as she gripped the receiver, listening closely to the officer. He proceeded to state that he was sorry to report an automobile accident involving her husband on Route 22, about three miles from their home. Her husband was taken to the Indiana

Hospital with a compound fracture of his skull and was pronounced dead at 3:05 p.m. by Dr. George Hanna. After hanging up, probably in shock, she immediately called her parents. Mary Lois Yelenic was a young bride, a new mother, and now in an instant . . . a widow!

Because of her strong religious faith, she knew she had to go on. Providing for herself and her infant son became her mission in life. Returning to her profession as an elementary education teacher, Mary Lois was able to keep money flowing into the household to pay for living expenses. John was watched each day by his aunts and Emma, his nanny, until school was dismissed and his mother returned home.

Mary Lois kept John busy during his formative years, involving him in his studies, music, drama, Boy Scouts and community work. She never remarried. She focused on John, her teaching, and maintaining a good home life. Holidays such as birthdays, Christmas, and Easter were always celebrated with decorating the house, cooking and filling their home with family and friends. There were dozens of albums full of photos to document the good times that they shared throughout the years.

John also kept albums full of photos of his son JJ growing up. I glanced through several that were on the coffee table in John's living room and on the dining room table. He indeed carried on the family tradition to pass it on to his son, JJ. Perhaps John was glancing through the albums the evening of April 12, 2006, with hope in his heart knowing the next day he would sign his divorce papers and his life would change.

Mary Lois held a tight rein on John as a young boy. Perhaps a little too tight. But that's understandable when you're a single parent. You can get fearful. Possibly John felt her loss compounded with the void of a father figure in his life. That would surely make anyone sad carrying these feelings around with them throughout the years. Everyone copes with sorrow differently. Some in positive ways while others find negative ways. John's way was being kind hearted, calming, and a friend to everyone he met. We have all met individuals like him in our lives.

The second person in this triangle is Michele Magyar-Kamler-Yelenic.

I found Michele to be the *tour de force* and then some. Every time her name came up in an interview, the interviewee would state how evil she was. "You could see it in her eyes," they would say. So after reviewing a number of Michele's pictures I found them to be correct. There was something about her wide, penetrating icy blue eyes.
Again after examining her parent-child relationship with the assistance of her brother John Magyar's interview in August of 2007, I began to understand how and why she became so deceitful, skillful, and shrewd. Every spirit has an internal flame. Some flutter softly giving off light and warmth. While others sit ablaze just waiting to strike out. Michele Magyar-Kamler-Yelenic, now thirty-nine years old, makes the Santa Ana fires of California seem like a bon fire when she gets even. Nothing is left standing but the remains of the fallen. Here's how she began her rampage against the world.
Michele was born June 9, 1971, to Elizabeth (Betty) and John Magyar Sr. in Johnstown, Pennsylvania. At age two her parents divorced. Her father moved out leaving Betty with a four-year-old daughter and a six-year-old son to raise. John Magyar, Jr. (her brother), became the

man of the house at a early age. Trying to become a protector and peacemaker. Knowing only too well that Michele undermined their home life with her pranks. Causing more chaos to the existing dysfunctional family setting.

The parent-child relationship he remembered was one of seeing his mother getting beaten down emotionally day in and day out. The divorce left him in the middle of a workaholic mother trying to keep the rent paid and food on the table. Their absent father went on with his life, remarrying and fathering another child. However, John remained in close contact with his father. With all the diversities going on around him, he managed to focus on graduating from high school and enrolling in college. As a resident of Arizona he has maintained a successful life as an engineering consultant, husband, and father.

According to John who firmly believes that fifty percent of the marriages today that end in divorce doesn't mean that all children turn out bad. "Some kids are just bad eggs," he said. Which is how he described his sister, Michele. His mother gave into her demands because she was the baby of the family. Or was Betty more or less scared of Michele's explosive behavior when she didn't get her way? Screaming, yelling, and breaking things only increases when gone uncorrected. By the time a youngster reaches those pre-teen years, the psychological profile is formed to a degree.

Michele Magyar became *idée fixe*. In business for Michele Magyar. The family triangle (father, mother, and offspring) didn't exist here other than in the Magyar name they shared. Genuine love and respect which bonds a family together was lacking. A custodial parent-child relationship had formed. Not to say Betty didn't love children because she was very hurt when Michele forbid

JJ from visiting her in 2005 while the molestation case against John Yelenic was in process. The reason was because Betty truly liked John. Not for a second would she be convinced that he would have done anything to harm his son. However, Betty knew only too well of her daughter's keen capability of persuasion. After all Betty's weakness gave Michele Magyar-Kamler-Yelenic all the more power in the world she needed to become the person she is today!

The third person in this triangle is Kevin James Foley.

Born May 30, 1965, in Hempstead, New York, he and his twin sister Karen were adopted by Gail and Kenneth Foley. I spoke to Gail Foley over the phone for several months during 2008 at her daughter Karen's home in Jefferson, Georgia. We first met in person at Kevin's bail hearing February 19, 2008, at the Indiana courthouse where he was being held for the murder of Dr. John Yelenic. I'll never forget how Kevin looked over his shoulder numerous times back at Gail who was sitting two rows behind him in the courtroom, just smiling at her as if to say . . . I'm in trouble but don't worry. I could see the pain on her face as she smiled back to him with reassurance.

They say a mother's love is unconditional and that was evident to me. Gail Foley wasn't going to let her son stand alone. I felt that their bond was unique, especially after speaking with her. I got the impression Kevin was the apple of her eye. On one hand, she was proud of her son achieving State Police status while in complete *DENIAL* of him becoming so enraged (with a knife in hand) to commit such an act as murdering another human being in cold blood. Would any mother want to concede to that reality?

Gail and Kenneth Foley were familiar with the adoption process since they had already adopted a boy they named James when he was very young. By 1967 Gail was ready to expand her family giving Jimmy another sibling.

A set of twins (boy and girl) were born to a young ill-equipped couple who could not provide a secure home for their infants. With no other choice than a painful one they placed them with an adoption agency. It just so happened to be the one the Foley family had dealt with in the past. When Gail became aware of the twin's plight, she wanted to see them. It was explained to her by the social worker involved with the case that the young children were living in a home with little food, untidy, dirty clothing, and parents who were very young and unable to even take care of themselves, let alone two little ones.

After reviewing several photos taken upon their placement, she could see the similarity the twins had to her. Their light blond hair, fair complexion, freckles, bright eyes, and petite frame resembled Gail to a tee. Not being able to bear separating the twins, she convinced her husband Kenneth to adopt them both. There was enough drama in their little lives in just twenty-four months that she just couldn't put them through anymore. Gail may have been petite in size but she was determined to give those babies a good, happy, home. Growing up in a blended family, Kevin understood the advantages and disadvantages only too well. Little did he imagine that one day he too would repeat the adoption route.

So in 1967 the adoption was finalized, giving the twins a new name, parents, brother, and home. They became known as Karen Foley and Kevin James Foley. Moving about hundred miles away from an urban life in Hempstead, New York, to the upstate lake resort community of Massapequa. Which is where the Foley family settled to begin a new chapter in their lives.

By now Gail had her hands full. Coming from a large family herself she felt most comfortable with all the excitement around the house. Physically the twins adapted to their new mother, father, and brother. With Gail's soft, caring, and loving ways she tried to repair the damaged parent-child relationship the twins had been exposed to in their short two year lifetime. Or could it ever be restored?

In a normal parent-child relationship, by age two the union is strong. You know your child's likes, dislikes, wants, needs, and so forth. He can run, climb, talk, cooperates, and still naps. But by two and a half the child's behavior changes. Their wants become known loud and clear. Being understood by others relieves much of the furious exasperations which he or she felt earlier when they could point and cry hoping someone knows what they wanted. Was Gail prepared to handle little Karen and Kevin not knowing that their early years of development were far from normal? She, too, had to adjust to each twin separately because they were at different levels of behavior management. Also factor in the gender card.

I learned that Kenneth Foley's rearing issues weren't as soft spoken as his wife, Gail's. Over the phone, I interviewed several individuals who knew of the Foley family in the Lake Schroon area. One in particular was an elementary school teacher and his wife who remembered young Kevin. While at school functions and local restaurants, they observed Mr. Kenneth Foley displaying usual loud, harsh, and overbearing outbursts toward his children. So many adjustments can overload a young child's coping mechanism. Sooner or later it's meltdown time. Who will pay the ultimate price for the actions of a lost child when he or she becomes mentally and physically capable of taking matters into their own hands?

CHAPTER TWO

*Deep in the corners of the mind
what one believes to be true,
either is true or it becomes the truth.*

When looking up the definition for adolescence in the dictionary the word *transition* jumps right out at the reader. Puberty, popularity, getting a driver's license, and parents are monumental to the average teenager's lifestyle. For boys they approach adolescence around fourteen and at twenty-five manhood. Girls begin at age twelve and reach womanhood at twenty-one. While reviewing a number of books on adolescence the general age is common, however, the individual reaching adolescence varies. The diversification could stem back to the *nature* versus *nurture* theory. Was the adolescent's genetic composition and home environment in sync? At least enough to prepare him or her for the emotional roller coaster ride of peer pressure and raging hormones which also accompany adolescence? Most teens will just grin and bear it, hopefully finding themselves still standing to tell about their experiences to others. Then there are some who lose their bearings along the way through "The Rite of Passage," just trying to avoid the worst consequences any adolescent can experience . . . isolation and vulnerability. Pressure from all directions (home, school, friends) can jolt a stable teen, let alone one who is on shaky ground to begin with. How do they cope with it all?

Did the parents do their job during early childhood by teaching their child morals and ethics so they are able to make good choices? By adolescence all the yes' and no's should be instilled in their consciences. If confronted with a choice, the teen should be able to determine what is the right and what is the wrong action to take. Sure they will challenge them but again *choice* is involved in the reasoning process. They should be asking themselves . . . are my judgments for the betterment of myself as well as for others? A conscience leads to good choices. Without a conscience, right from wrong doesn't mean a thing.

Mary Lois kept her son John on the straight and narrow path throughout his teen years while making his way through high school. According to his academic records he was a member of the National Honor Society, Who's Who, and Student of the Month, to list a few achievements. He also participated in student council, prom committee, Civil War club, numerous plays, and the marching band. Keeping a well-balanced school career was a priority in the Yelenic home. Discipline paid off with a high grade point average. During an interview with John's physical education teacher, Albert Dettore stated, "John knew what he wanted to become at a very young age, a dentist. He worked very hard to accomplish his goal."

Looking through school yearbooks and family albums, John's life appeared full. Pictured participating in the highlights of high school life from proms to leads in the senior play, his world appeared normal. Even though he didn't have a father, his cousin Tracy Jacobs (who was eighteen years older than him) was like a big brother: spending time kicking around together, sharing holidays, family members' birthday parties, taking John hunting, and attending sporting events. Tracy and his wife, Judy were regulars at Mary Lois' home, helping with whatever she needed done, from home repairs to sharing Sunday dinners after church.

The good family values instilled in John by all the close-knit relatives became the driving force which compelled him to believe that he, too, would have his *own* family one day. He knew what a family meant. He knew what belonging felt like as well. After his education was finished and his dental practice was established, the stage would be set for the next step he would take . . . getting married. But for now, John had a long road ahead. College then dental school opened the doors to relocation, new friends, and challenges. With a strong foundation in moral values as well as John's resilience, he was well on his way to adulthood.

Insecurity impacted Michele Magyar's early years of development. Her mother Betty's personality (somewhat passive) was no match for Michele's aggressiveness, which grew out of giving in to Michele's demands during her early childhood. When a child is two or three, their actions are considered cute, and some parents tolerate bad behavior while hoping that the child will outgrow those habits. Perhaps just wishful thinking for parents who don't like using discipline? However, when the youngster reaches eleven and twelve (pre-teen) those habits have probably intensified along with their physical development.

With the absence of what a father figure represents in the family dynamics during Michele's emotional development, the odds were stacking up against her. She was lacking the control and confidence needed to develop into a well-adjusted young girl emotionally as well as mentally. Remember, all little girls are in love with their fathers. To them, their fathers are bigger than big and protect them from monsters, giving them unwavering love, security, confidence and so forth. Dads rule the home, which in turn becomes the family's safe haven from the outside world and everyone in it. Without him, what fills that void? Love, hate, anger, jealousy, aggression, bitterness? The void, therefore, falls upon the shoulders of the only other parent in the relationship to make life worth living. If the parent is not emotionally stable, then the results can be catastrophic for the youngster as he or she comes of age.

I interviewed her brother John Magyar, who turned out to have completed high school in good standing, graduated from college, and became a successful engineer. When asked about Michele's personality traits, he stated that she was impulsive, self-centered, and very immature. He remembered her running away from home at night by slipping out her bedroom window to meet up with her friends on the street. He would call his father up on the phone to come over to the house, and together they would go around the neighborhood looking for her. Only to bring her back home to repeat the procedure a day or so later. What was she running from or to? Did anyone ever ask her? Was this her way of getting her father's attention? By the tenth grade, Michele had reached the end of her patience with vocational classes and high school in general. At age sixteen she decided to drop out.

A few months later (1986) she married her high school sweetheart, Jeff Kamler. Together they had a daughter who they named Nicole Kamler. A son they named Nathan followed four years later. By 1990 the marriage was over. A divorce followed. Statistical data informs us time and time again that marriages among individuals so young lead to divorce due to such variables as maturity, education, employment, and finances to name a few. With those limitations, how can a young couple in their teens have a fair chance to succeed?

However, John Magyar did lead a normal life upon graduation from high school. He went on to college, married, relocated out of state (halfway across the United States), was employed, and was living at peace with himself. Then how do two children living in the same household, with the same mother develop such different lifestyles? When I asked John that question, he stated his teachers were his mentors. He was the oldest and was perhaps more serious as well as more observant while growing up. Observing, for example, how his mother was *fearful* of Michele's behavior. Which could explain why Betty has stood by her daughter. What about guilt? Now that's a great hook in the blame game to accept as a parent. If they don't accept the guilt then they, too, are in denial. Which is where John Magyar states his mother has remained in to date.

While moving through adolescence, Kevin Foley found sports as his outlet. He was an average student, quiet, and shy. His brother James, on the other hand, was popular and more outgoing with the other students. Due to the failing health of Mr. Kenneth Foley the family decided to sell the hotel and camping lodges which they owned and operated for several years. Relocating to a warmer climate became the answer to improving Mr. Foley's health. So the family settled in the state of Florida, near Fort Richey. By then Kevin was about ten years of age. He turned in his hockey skates and hockey games for running shoes and the track.

After completing high school, Kevin enlisted into the military, one way so many young men place their pasts behind and look forward to committing to yet another family as a member of the United States Army. Is that what Kevin yearned for in the first place . . . discipline or just getting lost within another system?

CHAPTER THREE

*A person can grow to his or her fullest potential
only in equally caring relationships with others.
If less then less it will be.*

Young adulthood is the time in one's life when we're guided by our goals in an uphill struggle to become a responsible citizen with the aim to advance mankind toward betterment. In accordance, John continued his education while meeting lifelong friends along his way whom he considered his brothers. Michele became a mother. Sometimes that changes a person's outlook on life from a negative to a positive. Kevin set out to join the Army. See the world like the advertisement goes.

As I delved into Michele and Kevin's lives during their twenties, red flags went up swaying in the air. There appeared to be undercurrents of trouble brewing. It was just a matter of time. When we're young we think time is on our side. There's always tomorrow as in *Gone With The Wind*. But unfortunately time waits for no one. The harsh realities will find you no matter where you try to hide.

By the late 1980s, John went on to dental school at the University of Pittsburgh. Michele was in her first marriage with Jeff Kamler residing in New Florence, PA. Kevin had just completed a four-year hitch in the Army and was now returning to Fort Richey, Florida, where his parents had been residing. He enrolled in the University of Florida while working part-time at a Walgreens drug store. He began dating Barbara Ray, a pharmacist whom he married and returned to her hometown of Ford City, PA, where her father owned Ray's Pharmacy.

When the early 1990s arrived, John had completed his dental degree and decided to move back to his hometown of Blairsville, PA. He could have gone into practice anywhere in the country, but he wanted to be close to his mother who was having health issues. Mary Lois financially backed John's dental practice. Her dream, hard work and sacrifice had paid off. John had become a dentist in the community she, too, had dedicated her life in as an elementary school teacher for thirty years. The Yelenic name meant honor and professionalism in Blairsville.

A second child had been born to Michele and Jeff Kamler, who they named Nathan. Their first child, Nicole, born in the late 1980s, now had a little brother to keep her company. Jeff was employed full time at the local tire company in Indiana. They were residing in a home that he had inherited from his parents. Jeff had everything in place for his young family to be comfortable. However, that lifestyle just wasn't enough to keep Michele content. A comfortable home, family, and steady income just didn't make Michele happy. Perhaps there was a *darker side* to this young, beautiful, twenty-something mother that would show its ugly face in due time. Yes, he took responsibility, but did Jeff Kamler really know what he had gotten himself into?

Don't get me wrong. Michele wasn't cooking gourmet dinners, knitting stockings and taking the children to the museum. Life was more like Ramen noodles: wear what you want and see you later, according to what John Magyar heard from conversations with Betty. Michele and Jeff divorced in the early 1990s. She relocated to Armstrong County, residing in a rented trailer at the West View Trailer Park along Plum Creek with Nicole and Nathan.

A series of live-in boyfriends moved in and moved out. I tracked down a few. Each one of them stated how sorry they felt for her children living like they did. That always puzzled me because these men had to have grown up in decent home environments to see that Michele wasn't conducting herself like a mother looking out for the well-being of her children. They were young men, in their twenties, with the desire to do what most guys do at that age . . . sow their oats. Some moved in with Michele and the children, with each relationship lasting between ten to fourteen months. As they ended the men moved out, some quietly in the dark of the night or simply thrown out by Michele. As one stated (C. Novack), "When Michele was through with you . . . you knew it." Still another odd statement was added by K. Kerr when I interviewed him. He had caught up with one of Michele's old boyfriends in a bar and they laughed about the realization that Michele had stolen their favorite t-shirts. Could it be a souvenir from the quest or solely a security (blanket) item? Maybe deep down Michele (the little girl) wanted to hold on to the scent of a male. Remember, Mr. Magyar left her just when little girls are in love with the father figure in their life.

Back when Michele was in the process of obtaining her divorce from Jeff Kamler in 1993 she met B. Gifford at a local bar. He had just been discharged after completing a tour of duty in Desert Storm. Upon returning home, he was trying to find employment. C. Novack informed me of an incident where Michele was arrested for plotting a scam with Gifford to go after an old girlfriend of one of the men Michele was involved with. This incident took her up to a new level of physical violence with intent of bodily harm creating a criminal record. I located the documented case (1993-0492-CRIM) at the Armstrong County Courthouse. The exact affidavit could not be located according to a court clerk. However she was able to provide me with a copy of the offenses for the both individuals involved:

*The affidavit was located months later

B.L. Gifford

Offense Date: 6-30-93   E 299902-1   #242
Charge: Terroristic Threats (cc2706) B.L Gifford

Offense Date: 7-26-93   E299910-2   #358
CHARGE: Aggravated Assault (cc2702-a-4)
 Simple Assault (cc2701-a-3)
 Recklessly Endangering Another Person (cc2705)
 Terroristic Threats (cc2706)

Gifford was ordered on April 5, 1994 to not less than 6 months nor more than 23 1/2 months at Armstrong Co. jail. September 28, 1994 he was released from incarceration at the Armstrong Co. jail on parole.

Michele (NMK) Kamler
Offense Date: 7-26-93 E 200013-5   #359
CHARGE: Conspiracy Aggravated Assault (cc2702-a-4)
Conspiracy Simple Assault (cc2701-a-3)
Simple Assault (cc2701-a-3)

Kamler was ordered on February 4, 1994 to be placed into a Accelerated Rehabilitative Disposition Program.

Filed: 1 year in program and 20 hours of community service.

I did make contact with Gifford who had turned his life around, was now married with two children and employed throughout the United States in the construction field. All of the men that I interviewed while probing into Michele's early years had married, had families, and always expressed how sad they felt for Nicole and Nathan. What those two young children had to endure during their formative years under the supervision of their mother had to have left emotional scarring, which they could be carrying around with them to this day as they enter into adulthood.

The only constant in Nicole and Nathan's life, from what I gathered, was not their father, but rather Michele's mother, Betty Stevens, who resides in Indiana, PA. Betty did remarry to a man who had adult children of his own. One thing I learned about Betty was that she was a hard worker, always trying to keep a paycheck coming in. At the same time, she kept one eye out for jobs to keep Michele working, too.

During Betty's employment at the Inn Towner Motel on Wayne Avenue in Indiana, PA, she worked her way up to the position of manager of the small motel. Allen Heath owned the motel as well as Uncle Sudsy's, a beer distributorship and sandwich shop on the adjoining property in the college town. One day Heath asked Betty if she knew anyone he could hire to help in the shop. She knew she could keep a closer eye on Michele if she could get her to take the job.

Michele was hired in the shop/beer distributorship according to Heath's records (which he and his wife documented and handed over to me when I interviewed them) from April 1994 to the end of December 1996. I found that intriguing because Michele Kamler was on probation as of February 4, 1994. Why was she employed in a store that sold alcoholic beverages? Even better than that . . . she went around to other bars in the area for Budweiser's "The King of Beers" promotions in *their* mini-dress, introducing new beers to customers. Several photos were found at John Yelenic's home of Michele inside and outside of one of the Inn Towner Motel rooms (# 7) wearing not one but three different colored mini-dresses with the name Budweiser down the front side of the garment and even posing on the bed. But this wasn't the first time Michele was a star.

I was told by Dave, a former Sheetz employee who worked with Michele (also in Indiana, a few blocks away), that Michele posed for life-sized photos with items sold at Sheetz that hung from the ceiling at their store and at others in the area. So Michele was at the height of her career by the mid 1990s. She was a man magnet with long curly black hair, tan, blue eyes, and slender figure. How could any man resist?

CHAPTER FOUR

While one person hesitates because he feels powerless, the other is pre-occupied with mistakes and becoming triumphant.

By the mid 1990s, John, Michele and Kevin's lives had rebounded. John entered into a practice with the Reilly brothers in Blairsville. Their father, Frances C. Reilly had practiced dentistry in the community on Stewart Street for 42 years. So John was wise to join the established group, sharing expenses, and adding his patient base to the practice. The group of dentist and staff moved into a remodeled building on Market Street to accommodate the business growth.

John Yelenic had his career just where he wanted, even purchasing a house of his own on S. Spring Street just a few blocks from the practice as well as from his mother's home. Mary Lois beamed with happiness knowing John had returned to his hometown roots. He could have relocated anywhere in the United States or even a more progressive economic based region in

Pennsylvania to begin a dental practice, but he chose home and for that she was so pleased. Because after all Mary Lois was advancing in age with health issues becoming a huge concern now. John was all she had other than a few sisters who were also up in age.

One afternoon an old high school classmate of John's by the name of Brian Parsely arrived for his appointment. While John was cleaning Brian's teeth they got onto the subject of dating. John asked Brian if he knew of any good looking single girls. Brian who delivered produce for a wholesaler in Blairsville called LaMantes told him of a girl who worked at Uncle Sudsy's. He stated she was really built and had heard she was on the wild side. When I interviewed Brian he stressed he just thought they were joking around never dreaming John would marry her. "She was just the type you have fun with . . . hot." As I observed Brian's face and body language, I could see he felt guilty for even mentioning Michele to John. But who knew that John would venture up to Uncle Sudsy's in Indiana on his own to take a look for himself? When John returned he told his friends he had met his "Homecoming Queen". I'm sure she thought she found her "Golden Goose"!

John was eager to settle down like any man. He wished to get married and fill his home with love and joy. Unfortunately, John had attracted someone who had another agenda in mind. How do you warn or protect a friend of possible danger without losing their friendship ? This was the position John's friends Tim, Dennis, Maggie, and Dr. Maria found themselves in upon hearing of all the hardships Michele thrust upon John beginning in 1999 through 2006.

An instant family was just what John was looking for. He wanted the excitement of family life. Remember

John was an only child yearning for a full house of people. To keep the group closer to Blairsville instead of driving back and forth to Indiana (where Michele was residing), he bought a building on Main Street which had a deli business on the first floor. With Michele's experience at Uncle Sudsy's, she with Betty's help with a few employees continued to run the business. The store was called The Main Street Deli. On the second floor was a large apartment where she, Nicole, and Nathan lived.

The deli business venture lasted from January 1997 to March 1997. Yes, only three months according to spreadsheets and banking statements which Mary Ann Clark discovered in a box at John's home. Records confirmed that the business was running in the RED from the start. While John was pouring thousands of dollars into it for utilities, purchasing products, and payroll each month. No one really worked the business or it could have survived. It was in a great location on a busy main street of downtown Blairsville with walk in traffic from both directions. Once again Betty was at Michele's side to assist. I noted that Betty always accumulated the most working hours in the payroll column. She probably couldn't believe John would give them such an opportunity as owning a business which is why Betty was willing to give her all. Unfortunately the novelty must have worn off with Michele. There were other doors opening for her now.

Towards the end of March John had received news that his mother's cancer had re-emerged. Mary Lois' sisters, her niece Judy Jacobs, and a visiting nurse cared for her in shifts around the clock. John would come every day after work to assist well into the morning hours. Soon Michele insisted on taking over the duties during the day since by now she wasn't working. So she relieved the visiting nurse by firing her and offended Judy, then told the sisters she was in charge sending them home too. With all the commotion going on John must have been overwhelmed just trying to keep his head above water with the practice yet alone seeing Mary Lois deteriorating.

    There were two notebooks that the caregivers recorded all the feedings, medications, changes of clothing and so forth for Mary Lois during her illness. It is easy to notice the difference in care from the time Michele came aboard. Her handwriting was a sure give away. It was larger, clearer as each letter in a word was written in a flowing precise fashion. I had compared her notes in the book to the checks she wrote out for the deli. They say the style of handwriting can give the onlooker insights to the personality of the writer. I was taken by it. The stereotype for a tenth grade dropout would probably be scribbling of some sort. That result wasn't found here. But the level of care wasn't as perfect as the handwriting she displayed. As her sisters continued to visit they too noticed the diapers weren't changed as often nor was the patient's face cleaned after a feeding. Everyone tried to help as much as they could without getting Michele upset for fear she would take it out on Mary Lois or tell John, adding even more heartache. However, Mary Lois' condition deteriorated quickly under mysterious circumstances.

    They say while the cat's away the mice will play or check things out while home alone. While it just so happened that Mary Lois had a life insurance policy and her will tucked away in one of the desk drawers. The amount of the life insurance policy was one million dollars with her son John the beneficiary. Could this discovery be just another motivating factor to marry John as soon as possible? After all Michele's no fool. Mary Lois passed away a few weeks later (May 1997). By the end of June, John re-wrote his will placing Michele Magyar-Kamler . . . yes, beneficiary. They weren't even married. However, John did move Michele and the children into his Spring Street home. Placing his mother's home up for sale, as well as the building the deli was in trying to reduce all the cost in maintaining the properties. John and Michele did marry in December 1997 in Las Vegas. Closing out the year of 1997.

CHAPTER FIVE

*While slowly descending down a dark tunnel,
the bottom appears closer than you think.*

By all the measurements of success . . . marriage, a comfortable home, financial security, and good health one would consider themselves the luckiest person on the face of the earth. But the honeymoon was quickly wearing off for John. Michele couldn't stand the lifestyle he was providing for her in Blairsville. Nicole and Nathan were having a great time in school and making friends with all the neighborhood children. With all the money John was making as a dentist why should they be sitting in little old Blairsville? So she set out to find them a mega-mansion in an upscale area of Indiana. White Farm Township was where the upper class crest of Indiana's society resided with their manicured lawns, fancy cars, and their children enrolled in private schools. That was the perfect location to begin another chapter of her life.

Michele found her dream house at 880 White Farm Road, consisting of four bedrooms, several stained glass windows throughout the house, three bathrooms, game rooms, a in-ground pool, surrounded by a two level deck on a two acre lot. Plenty of space to have a hockey rink designed for Nathan to practice on. This was a big step up in the world for someone who had been on welfare just a few months before. Yes, Michele worked her magic on John and won.

For John the house was bigger than he could imagine. Once telling his old college buddy Dennis Vaughn that the only place he felt comfortable in the house at 880 White Farm Road, was in the smallest of the two furnace rooms. Spending large sums of money didn't just stop at the purchasing of their mega-mansion. Other rental properties in the area were being purchased, such as a four unit apartment building for Michele to manage, as well as those in Blairsville. Yes, money was flowing in all directions for lavish vacations, furniture, landscaping, clothing, diamond jewelry, and into Michele. Yes, Michele! Body altering was where she needed to focus on now. So she made her plastic surgery appointment for breast implants as well as buttock shaping. Not to mention numerous tattoos. It wasn't too hard to convince John to invest in her appearance. Michele was high maintenance. After all she was what dreams are made of.

On the other hand, John wanted something out of the deal too. He wanted to become a father. They tried numerous times however, Michele could not get pregnant. Unbeknown to John was the fact that she had had her tubes tied years ago. She knew she had to come up with a solution and quickly. *Adoption!* Immediately she began searching internet adoption sites. During the 1990s, adoptions from Russia were very prevalent, costing as high as thirty thousand dollars or more. A little Russian boy caught Michele's eye while surfing various adoption sites. She remembered John telling her that the Yelenic's had Croatian roots, and she was convinced this Russian baby boy would be the key in keeping her connected to John . . . and the money. John couldn't wait to make the arrangements for all of them to travel to Russia and adopt the infant. Within a few weeks all the paperwork and funds were transferred. John, Michele, Nicole, and Nathan went to Moscow to pick up their newest addition to the Yelenic family.

Michele was showered with cards, presents, and money from John's family and friends. The little boy was eighteen months old and was named John Jay Yelenic, Jr. Finally, Michele was firmly bonded to John. The certificate of birth issued March 31, 2003 by the Commonwealth of Pennsylvania's Department of Health (vital records # FB 15344-1998) confirmed Michele Magyar-Yelenic as his mother. It couldn't get any better than that, or could it and for whom?

The first thing Michele did was place JJ in day care. She didn't work but needed time for herself. The whole family scene—supper on the table, cleaning the house, paying bills and keeping the show going—wasn't happening for John. Betty would, at times, step in to help while his wife was out with her friends. Before he knew what hit him Michele decided a separation was in order and demanded that he move out. Rather than place any more stress on the children's home life, he consented.

A dominate personality, such as the one Michele had, naturally overpowered John, who his friends would define as that of an easy-going big teddy bear. He walked around in shock, according to my interview with his dental assistant of thirteen years, Joyce Cucciado. Joyce expressed how heartbreaking it was to watch John floundering. She never forgot the day in the office when he admitted to her that he should have listened to her advice and not marry Michele. But it was too late. Michele had dug in and wasn't going to let go come hell or high water. A few weeks later Joyce's husband was transferred out of state due to his job. She followed a few months later after selling their home. Knowing she was leaving John at a time when his life was in so much chaos overwhelmed her so much emotionally that it still brought tears to her eyes on the day of our interview.

    John moved out of his Indiana home in 2001, returning to Blairsville. Since his house at 233 S. Springs Street was leased out at the time, he rented a trailer in the area until the lease was up. Then he moved back in. Michele and the children remained in the White Farm Road house until 2002. At that time they relocated to Johnstown, PA where her new boyfriend S. Glosser (soon to become her fiancé) resided. How she meet him, I'm not sure. Some say Michele met him on the internet; others say she was introduced to him by a friend.

    Oddly enough while all this was transpiring, she was still legally married to John Yelenic. Financial support was being forwarded to her and the kids from John, but she insisted on no physical connection with him. Records show a protection from abuse order against him was filed by her in the Cambria County Courthouse (Johnstown) in 2003. Many saw this to be Michele's way of discontinuing John's right to have visitations with his son. I guess what better way than to establish a molestation issue. After all, according to her brother John Magyar, Michele and his ex-wife tried it on him, and it worked even though it was false. The results were devastating for John Magyar and difficult for any man to comprehend it happening to them. It took Magyar years to get over losing any opportunity of forming a future relationship with his daughter.

What goes around comes around. Now Michele had another problem materializing right before her eyes with S. Glosser's mother. Who insisted on Michele signing a pre-nuptial agreement since the Glosser family was very well to do in the retail business. They owned several large department stores in the downtown business district of Johnstown. There was no way Michele was signing off. So she kept the ring until Saul's family attorney forced her to return it. There are even some who state she kept it. Who knows for sure whatever became of the ring? Things were going downhill from there for Michele. Next, she was instructed to move out of Saul's residence. With nowhere to go Michele contacted John to bail her out by stating his son JJ needed a home or he'd be living out in the streets. Furthermore, she told him, there was no way she would bring herself and the kids back to Blairsville.

Meanwhile, John had been in negotiations throughout the summer of 2003 with a real estate agent to finalize the selling of the White Farm house. Now under more pressure, he took a two hundred thousand dollar loss just to get out from under it, so he could obtain the needed funds to purchase another home before the school year began for the children. Again, in another fashionable neighborhood of Indiana, Michele found a suitable house on Susan Drive. John paid cash for it, placing the deed in Michele Yelenic's name. It doesn't get any better than that. What was John thinking? Once again Michele lands on her feet like a cat with nine lives. She was back in her old stomping grounds with Betty close enough to get dinner on the table and the household running smoothly, and Jeff Kamler and John sending their child support checks monthly. I could only think about what her brother John Magyar stated in his interview: "Michele liked to have the checks coming so she didn't have to work. Just keep the check coming".

    Trying to juggle his estranged wife's demands, maintaining some form of family normality and security for JJ (Nicole and Nathan), and satisfying his partner Tom Reilly (by increasing patient numbers at the dental practice), took its toll on John physically. He gained weight due to taking anti-depressants, drinking, and eating junk food. Tim, Dennis, Maggie, and Maria tried to keep in close contact with John with daily phone calls and visits. Seeing their dear friend in his present condition, their concerns continued to escalate from 2004 to 2006. They wanted him to relocate near one of them. He could practice dentistry anywhere. But John would not leave, knowing JJ would not have his real father in his life. That feeling of guilt must have been the driving force for him to stick it out no matter what happen to him.

    While John's life was in total shambles Kevin Foley wasn't batting a hundred either. He was unhappy with his choice to work as a delivery driver at the pharmacy where Barbara was working. He wanted to pursue his criminology career since he had already received a bachelor's degree from the University of South Florida before they relocated to Pennsylvania. He enrolled at the Indiana University of Pennsylvania, about fifteen miles from their home in Ford City/Leechburg area. Applying to the Act I Program for Pennsylvania State Police, he passed all his classroom and training requirements. His name was added onto a list of candidates awaiting appointment to a barracks. By 1994 his career was underway as he was assigned to the Indiana Barracks of the Pennsylvania State Police.

In the marriage department, Barbara and Kevin began to drift apart. Why? Perhaps because Kevin yearned for a family of his own. It was brought out later during his trial that Barbara was physically unable to give birth and had suffered several miscarriages throughout the years. Kevin filed for divorce in 1997, but withdrew it (perhaps to try again at parenthood). In 2000 he re-filed for divorce in Armstrong County. Once the divorce was granted, he moved out of their home and signed off on the deed, placing it back into Barbara Ann Ray's name. Kevin moved back into the town of Indiana.

A few years later, Kevin meet a beautiful blond-haired woman by the name of S. Smith who was employed at a local bank. She was still living with her parents in their family home, which may have convinced him of her stability. They married in 2002 and a large wedding photo appeared in the *Indiana Gazette*. This marriage lasted from September 7, 2002, until June 8, 2003.

Once again Kevin filed for a divorce. When I pulled their marriage and divorce paperwork at the Indiana Courthouse, I was surprised to discover that Sue's attorney put up quite a fight to get Kevin to adhere to alimony payments. Yes, alimony! For a marriage that lasted less than a year (eight months), Kevin was ordered to pay spousal support that began on December 18, 2003, and ended on June 27, 2004. The amount of each payment was $622.00. With court cost and extras the amount increased to $702.00 per month.

Kevin remained in their home on Charles Street. Sue returned to her family home. I never understood why Kevin was the one filling for divorce in both cases. What

I did know is neither Barbara nor Sue would give me the time of day. They hung up every time I mentioned Kevin Foley's name. Perhaps his exes didn't want any repercussions from the local police nor the State Police. Whatever the reason, Kevin was able to build a reputation among his co-workers and acquaintances as a person of power. An enforcer like that can intimidate whomever they wish whenever they wish to do so. Remember, there's always someone who pays the price for power.

It took me quite a while to get to the source of how Michele Magyar-Kamler-Yelenic and Kevin Foley met. No one really knew or would give it up. But on March 19, 2009, at Kevin's trial, his attorney Richard Galloway asked that question. Kevin explained that he accompanied a fellow crime investigations officer to 10 Susan Drive in Indiana to follow up on a complaint filed against Michele by a boyfriend. The boyfriend accused her of hacking into his computer and using his personal information. It was at that point contact was made, leading up to a friendship which later turned into a so-called romance. By the close of 2003 Kevin moved into her home. Now Michele had her own private bodyguard, another financial backer to keep the money flowing, a built-in babysitter and, best of all, JJ was told to call him "Daddy," while Nicole and Nathan could refer to Kevin as "Trooper."

This dysfunctional family dynamic was the farthest definition of family John could have ever imagined. Think about it for a minute. Michele came from a divorced home life, and Kevin didn't even know who his real father and mother were. While being adopted into another family at age two. Nicole and Nathan knew they had Jeff Kamler at the beginning of their childhood as their father. Then a series of Michele's boyfriends strolled in and out of their lives. Finally, John Yelenic arrived only to be pushed out of the picture right when they were experiencing the closest to a normal (secure) family life they ever had. By the time they were in their teens in comes Kevin Foley. JJ was not yet five years old when he was told that he now had a "new daddy." Call this stranger (Kevin) "Daddy," who had just moved in? I don't think even Mother Theresa could sort this nightmare out. Two negatives don't make a positive. Only time would prove that theory. Tick-tock, tick-tock!

CHAPTER SIX

When in a dilemma how one resolves the problem reflects upon his/her character.

Out of all the relationships Michele has had throughout her life, the one she maintained with Kevin was the longest, next to that of Betty Magyar, her mother. I debated for some time whether Kevin's role was that of her bodyguard or her handler. Who was doing all the thinking? Was it Michele, a tenth grade dropout, or Kevin, the state trooper crime investigator? While studying this murder mystery over the years, one suspects it could have been either a series of coincidences or a strategic, well-thought-out scheme.

One afternoon while I was thumbing through folders a sheet of paper fell to the floor. It was the "Action For Custody Complaint" form. Jeffrey J. Kamler was the plaintiff who filed against Michele Yelenic (defendant) back on March 27, 2002, in the Court of Common Pleas of Indiana County, Pennsylvania (no. 10512).

The core of the issue was Nicole's desire to live with her father. However, since the child was only fourteen and had lived with her mother for years, "Children in the Middle'"—a comprehensive education program for divorcing parents—was recommended by the judge. Both Michele Magyar-Kamler-Yelenic and Jeffery Kamler attended the counseling program which resulted in their receiving a certificate of completion. This satisfied the court. Did the parents ever comprehend the seriousness of the emotional problems Nicole, Nathan, or JJ were trying to cope with as kids of divorced/separated parents? Did anyone care?

Nicole continued living with her mother until she graduated from high school. Making a break, she decided to apply to a business school in Pittsburgh and enroll in a two year veterinary assistant program. During the summers, she remained in Pittsburgh employed at a retail shop while visiting Indiana now and then. Did she have any revelations of what was to be in the future pertaining to Dr. John Yelenic? Did she hear anything through the grapevine? After all, Nicole was no stranger to e-mail and Facebook.

The Indiana County courtrooms weren't unfamiliar places to Michele. If she didn't know all the judges there, surely Trooper Kevin Foley might have since he was a crime investigator for the state police. One of the most horrifying situations John was confronted with took place in the fall of 2005 when a second PFA charge was filed against him. Only this time it stemmed from many under current reasons.

First and foremost, John helped many of his friends and employees financially, which drove Michele nuts. She couldn't stand John just giving away his earnings . . . because of course that meant less for Michele's needs. It had to stop and fast! She just had to find a way to get his attention. Now, you have to remember John was a simple no-frills type of person according to his friend Dennis Vaughn and his cousin Mary Ann Clark. If extra money could assist someone who was in a tight situation financially, John was there to help with no questions asked. Maybe it was a fault, but he was a loyal friend in every sense of the word. That might have really eaten away at Michele, even though John was paying thousands of dollars in support payments, school tuitions, hockey expenses, and so forth. I guess there is never enough.

Money was one issue that annoyed her while the other was sharing custody of JJ. The staged visitation meetings to transfer JJ over to John were anything but smooth going. Most of the time Kevin was present, which just added to the commotion. On one occasion they gave John the wrong time to meet, which led to him arriving an hour late. Another time, JJ was so worked up that he carried on during the transfer by screaming, kicking, spitting at John, and crying out that he didn't want to go. What was the purpose of all that? Did Michele hope that John would just drive off and not take JJ? And thereby showing the child that his father really didn't want him? John probably tried to do the best he could under the circumstances by taking JJ to get something to eat.

Once, after JJ returned from a visitation during the fall of 2005, Michele contacted the Blairsville police to report what JJ had told her. She claimed that JJ pointed to the areas of his body that John touched. A molestation charged was filed with the Indiana Courthouse and CYS against John Yelenic. This led to arrangements being made with the local Blairsville Police Department to proceed immediately with his arrest. Wearing his work scrubs, Dr. John Yelenic was handcuffed then escorted past the seated patients in the waiting room, through the front doors of the building to a police vehicle parked at the curb. That surely had to be one of the lowest points in his life. Could he ever rebound from that? Maybe he was now realizing Michele's plan. Shortly after Michele filed for separation back in 2002, the chain of events leading up to this 2005 encounter had been in the works. Many of his family and friends believed Dr. John Yelenic knew he was a *dead man walking* as far back as 2002. While others maintained it was the moment he set eyes on his *Homecoming Queen* back in 1995.

Friends, family, and employees couldn't comprehend the charges against John. It was completely out of character. How could anyone come up with such a story? John hired attorney Sam Reigh from Pittsburgh, PA, to defend him. He had been referred to him by Effie Alexander who was working on John's divorce papers. Sam asked John to take a polygraph, which he agreed to do immediately. He had nothing to hide and wanted the truth to be known that he was no child molester. John was administered the test in Punxsutawney, PA, by a polygraph expert in the area. This kept the entire procedure on a neutral basis, since it was out of Indiana County where the polygraph testing would be done by state police personnel. In John's case, it was wise for his attorney to direct the test be taken out of the area. According to the interview I did with Attorney Reigh in September 2007, Dr. Yelenic was informed that he had passed with flying colors.

Now they had to get to the root of this claim. When JJ was privately questioned by Judge Carol Hanna of the Indiana County Court during the hearing, JJ admitted to the judge that his mother told him to say his father touched him in his private areas during a visitation. Betty Magyar also attended the hearing and was called as a character witness for Dr. Yelenic. She confirmed that he was an honorable person, and that in all the years she knew him, nothing like this was ever mentioned nor noticed. I was told by persons who attended the trial in support of John that, when it ended, Michele was heard throughout the hallway (outside of the courtroom), telling Betty that she was forbidden to see the children since she had sided with John. Of course, that only lasted until Michele needed Betty to babysit or come over to cook for them.

It was reported to me by several witnesses that Kevin and a fellow state trooper sat in their seats during the trial, smiling and blowing kisses to John while he was in the witness seat under oath giving his testimony. When John, a Seinfeld fan, stepped down to returned to his seat, he turned and gave Kevin the noted Seinfeld sign. Of course, Judge Hanna noticed that, which lead to her citing John for disorderly conduct. I thought it was odd that Judge Hanna never noticed Kevin and his sidekick out in the audience facing the witness stand and acting up while John was testifying.

It all boiled down to Michele falsely fabricating a molestation case in an attempt to prevent John from attending a 2005 dental convention in Florida. Dr. Maria Tacelosky, a friend of John's who attended dental school with him, was going to be there with her husband and two children. So he thought it would be a great way to enjoy a peaceful fun time all together. Michele hated the idea. She especially hated Dr. Maria because she always felt John had a thing for her. According to Michele, John had a thing with every woman he came in contact with. Why would she even care? She had been seeing other men. Even living with Kevin Foley since 2004. So she took matters into her own hands and had JJ's hair shaved down to a very close buzz cut, dressed him as a girl, with lipstick and rouge and packed his suitcase with girl's outfits. She placed him on the porch, just waiting for John to come by to pick him up for the trip. I wouldn't have believed it either, but pictures don't lie. I couldn't help but notice how tired and drained John appeared. Little did he know that even more stress was coming his way upon his return home to Blairsville.

When John met Roberta Mack (Bobbi), a single mother, at the ice hockey games, his life was beginning to look promising. Nathan began playing ice hockey at a young age, showing a remarkable talent in the sport as a goalie. Bobbi Mack's son and Nathan played on the same team, known in the league as the Badgers. While the games were being played, John and Bobbi enjoyed cheering for their sons as well as cups of hot chocolate. As time went on, they began seeing one another outside the hockey arena.

Bobbi was a special educational teacher, mature, realistic, kind, and loving and possessing all the qualities John could definitely relate to. They were even making plans for a future together, such as selling her home and relocating to another area to start fresh. For once John had a chance to finally have a normal home life. Then he could proceed to gain full custody of JJ. John felt a responsibility to be a good father; he just couldn't walk away leaving JJ at the mercy of Michele and Kevin like some thought he should. John wasn't raised to be that type of person. He knew what it was like to have a protective mother like Mary Lois was after his father had passed away. John wanted what was right.

Bobbi was taking care of her mother, who was ill, when she and John began seeing one another. One day, to Bobbi's surprise, she received a card in the mail. Not just any card, a sympathy card. It was from no other than Michele. A handwritten note was enclosed stating, "This is what will happen to you so keep away from John!" Meanwhile, John was receiving calls day and night from a screaming Michele, informing him that he wouldn't be seeing JJ anymore unless he stopped dating Bobbi. At the hockey games, Michele would wait until Bobbi arrived, then park so intentionally close to Bobbi's car that she couldn't get out of the driver's side. In mid-December, in an attempt to halt the harassment, John and Bobbi decided to end their relationship. During our interview, a tearful Bobbi expressed that her deepest regret was making that decision. There was no telling what scheme Michele had up her sleeve next. Bobbi had to look out for the safety of her son and herself.

By the Christmas season John must have reached rock bottom. His relationship with Bobbi ended. I was told by Mary Ann Clark that Michele wouldn't permit JJ and the other kids to visit John to help decorate the tree, which had been a family tradition, nor to receive the gifts he had bought and wrapped for them. He hoped Michele would have a change of heart and let the kids have their gifts. The packages sat in the living room next to the tree near the fireplace as the month of December ended and the New Year 2006 began. As a young boy growing up, Christmas and Easter were the highlight of John's years. Looking through several photo albums, it was obvious that the two holidays represented joyous times for John, Mary Lois, his cousin Tracy Jacobs, and family friends. John entered the world during the Lenten season in 1967. So how could his demise have taken place thirty-nine years later on Holy Thursday? Coincidence or a deeper plan?

Which brings me to a story John's dental assistant Joyce C. told me. While John was still married to Michele, she would prohibit him from bringing home any gifts he received from his staff for Christmas. Nor did she know he gave his staff gifts. Again John was spending money on THEM. Once she found out, in retaliation, Michele would go out and purchase diamond bracelets, necklaces and expensive designer clothes for herself and the children. Nothing but the best was her motto and he'll pay for it . . . she ruled.

With the New Year 2006 underway, the flood gates were now open. John contacted his attorney Effie Alexander and informed her to get the divorce proceedings going immediately. He allotted $3,700.00 per month for spousal alimony and child support, not only for his son JJ, but also providing for Nicole and Nathan. Does it get any better than that? Totaling $41,000.00 a year for being in a marriage (or just living together) from December 1997 to June 2001 or there about. Their separation began around 2001 and continued until his death on the night of April 12, 2006. He was to sign his **FINAL** divorce motion at 3:00 p.m. on Holy Thursday, April 13, 2006.

When Attorney Effie Alexander informed John around February of 2006 that he didn't have to pay for the other two children since Michele didn't want him to adopt them when he offered back in 2002, John was entitled to decrease the child support payment from $3,700.00 per month to $1,300.00 (less than half). When that notification was sent to Michele, the backlash began. Changes in the *martial settlement agreement* set the ball in motion by the start of March 2006.

More harassments developed as a result of the financial adjustment: John's car was spray painted while parked in front of his house, calls were made to his home and dental office, and his friends harassed. I guess, as the saying goes, payback is a bitch. John tried turning to the local Blairsville police, but all they could do was write up the incidents and give him a copy of the report. The state police from the Indiana barracks were the next law enforcement agency in the area. Trooper Kevin Foley was based there, so who could John turn to for help? He didn't want any of this friends or family members becoming entangled any further in this web nor harmed in any way. He wanted to protect them even though he himself was in more danger than he could ever imagine. I think he must have known he was doomed. The reason I allege that is because Dr. Yelenic asked Attorney Alexander to open up a fund to cover the cost of a private investigator should HE be found murdered.

By the end of March, a martial settlement agreement was reached between Attorney Effie Alexander and Michele's attorney, Daniel Lovette, from Johnstown. Those who knew of Michele's love of money couldn't believe she had agreed to the divorce if it wasn't to her advantage. Many were convinced that something was up. Perhaps Michele wanted to give John a feeling of false security, which would place him in a vulnerable position. She voluntarily agreed to sign the divorce papers with just one small adjustment on John's part. The adjustment (pertaining to rental property payment) was made and the document was then finalized and forwarded to him for his signature. Upon receiving the last part of the divorce agreements on April 8, 2006, John made arrangements with his Aunt Ruth and Uncle Hilding Carlson to witness his signing at a notary's office on his day off, and it was scheduled for Thursday, April 13, 2006. Wednesday evening, April 12, 2006, at 9:15 p.m., he called Aunt Ruth to confirm their meeting and expressed how happy and overwhelmed he was to finally be able to put all the hurt of the past nine years behind him. He felt a sense of exhilaration because the next day was to be the beginning of a new life for him.

So on John's day off from the dental practice, Thursday, April 13 at 3:00 p.m., Aunt Ruth, Uncle Hilding and his cousin, Mary Ann Clark, were waiting for him at the local notary's office in Blairsville to witness him sign the final divorce papers. John NEVER showed up!

CHAPTER SEVEN

Who we are inside is what helps us make and do everything in life. It's the courage to be ourselves.

This chapter is written from the victim's perspective.

Now here I am butchered to death. My lifeless body, laying in a pool of my own blood just waiting for someone to discover me. I knew that tragic day would come, but never thought it would happen in my own home on Holy Thursday. Wait a minute! Someone's jiggling the front door knob. Oh, no! I bet it's Zak trying to get in to return a tape he borrowed yesterday. Good, he stopped. The television is still on. Wait! Now I hear someone else at the front door. Jiggling it, too, only this time I can see an arm reaching in, trying to unlock the doorknob. It's Craig, Zak's older brother, entering the hallway and slowly walking towards me. Broken glass is everywhere. I can hear it crackling as he's walking closer to me. Stopping in front of my bloody body, he's gazing down. He must have noted that I'm not breathing. Looking back up, Craig is scanning the room.

Blood is splattered over the walls of the hallway, archway, living room, dining room, on furniture, and the fireplace. Papers and pictures are scattered all over the floor and covered in blood. I can see the hopelessness on his face, and know this murder scene will haunt him in the days, months and years to come. Shaking his head, he quickly turns and runs out the front door.

It's only a short time later, and Craig returns with his grandfather thinking he can help. At 3:25 p.m. Thursday, April 13, 2006, Tom Jennings makes the 911 call to the Blairsville Police Department alerting them of their findings at 233 S. Spring Street.

As the minutes pass, Tom Jennings and Craig move away from my body, being careful not to disturb anything around me. How I'll miss them. They were good people to me all the years I've known them. I can now hear fire sirens approaching in the distance, followed quickly by the sound of truck doors slamming. I know the drama is mounting. All the characters will be appearing one by one in the hours, days, weeks, and months to come. But my murderer will hide for now since the evil deed has been done.

In through the front door comes Cpl. Janelle Lydic of the Blairsville Police Department, another officer and the EMS. As soon as she observes the crime scene in the hall and living room, she orders everyone out of the house. Cpl. Lydic is going by the book and instructs the other officer to do a full search of the premises. He turns toward the steps leading up to the second floor bedrooms and immediately begins climbing up each step slowly. Cpl. Lydic's next move is to phone her boss, Chief Hess, at his home to alert him of the situation since his shift is over for the day. She leaves a message for him about my homicide. It's not a case of cardiac arrest, which she had been told on her original radioed communication. As procedure goes in such cases, she calls the Indiana County Coroner Mike Baker over to document my death and the removal of what is left of my bloody lifeless body.

    I don't know if my homicide was a surprise to Cpl. Lydic or not. My trouble over the years with Michele and her live-in boyfriend, Trooper Foley, was not new to Chief Hess or the police in Blairsville. THEY were the ones who answered Michele's numerous complaints. Even coming to my office to arrest me on her claims. I wonder if Cpl. Lydic put it together when she first heard the address, 233 S. Spring Street? Cardiac arrest. I wish. *Slaughtered* is more like it!

    Mike Baker arrives, and I know he will get the show moving. I can only imagine the crowd that must be forming on the street by now. Where were all these people when I was crying out in horror last night as I was being carved to death? They couldn't hear the argument, the yelling, my body (some 275 pounds) being thrown around the room—hitting walls, furniture overturning and me being pushed through a glass window head first then pulled back through? Come on . . . it was around midnight and lights were on in the neighborhood. My lights were on. Why didn't someone . . . anyone . . . call the police? The station is only a few blocks away. They could have been at my house within minutes. Someone could have possibly saved my life. Now here I am, on my way to the morgue. Mike bagged my hands, thank God!

    Poor Aunt Ruth and Mary Ann. They're probably going out of their minds worrying about where I am. They'll learn soon enough. Meanwhile, Mike has me at the morgue. He's examining me and documenting his findings. I can hear him talking on his phone, making arrangements to have me transported to Dr. Cyril Wecht's facility at Carlow University in Pittsburgh. Dr. Wecht is a world renown forensic pathologist. He'll be able to reveal what was happening to me during my final moments of life. I know I am in good hands, pardon the pun.

It's the next morning—Friday April 14, 2006 at 9:00 a.m. Dr. Cyril Wecht began my autopsy hours ago —poking, scraping, and clipping as he inspected every inch of my body, inside and out. I was basically in good health for a 39 year old male. My heart was in good shape for my age, I was cancer free, with no diseases found near or in my internal organs. The next question is why am I here? That's the million dollar question, I guess. Dr. Wecht noted the following on my death certificate as the two immediate causes of death: (a) Exsanguination, and (b) Lacerations of Head, Neck, Chest and Right Arm. The manner of death, he further ruled, was homicide. Then he sewed me closed, placed me in a black body bag, wheeled it to a hearse, laid it in, and off we went.

I was driven back to Blairsville. Only this time I reported to 49 N. Walnut Street in the hands of Richard Shoemaker, the funeral director who had also assisted in preparing my mother Mary Lois back in 1997. Now the arrangements were being made for me by my cousin Mary Ann Clark. She won't rest until my killers are brought to justice. That, she will learn, is not going to be an easy mission. She'll be up against Michele, Kevin Foley, the Indiana State Police, and Indiana County. They never showed any mercy for me. But I'm confident that, with the support of Tim Abbey, Dennis Vaughn, Mag McCartin, and Dr. Maria, they won't let up until my murderer(s) are arrested and convicted, no matter how long it takes. They know all about the torment I was put through leading up to this day. They're ready to do whatever they have to do to solve my homicide. As a father my soul aches knowing that my son JJ is now totally in the hands of the very ones who despised me while I was alive. Michele never even brought JJ to the funeral home nor sent flowers. How can my soul ever find peace, or will I just roam the earth?

Seeing me laid out in a coffin has to be shocking to my family, friends, employees, and patients. I was surprised to hear that when the funeral director, Richard Shoemaker, called Michele for arrangements he was told, "Do what you want with his body." Did I expect anything less from Michele? Mary Ann and her daughter ran around to a secondhand thrift shop searching for a black turtleneck shirt for me to wear. That helped cover up all the stitches around my neck that the funeral director made in an attempt to hold my head in the right position on my shoulders! "Do what you want with his body." Thanks, Michele.

On the way to the cemetery I could see a long line of cars trailing behind the hearse. As the hearse slowly drove through the cemetery it finally came to a stop. It was at a grave site only too familiar to me. It was my grandparents. Next to it, was a opening large enough to fit the coffin down into the dark cold earth with three tons of dirt on top. It was my destination. How could this have happened to me? I was a loving son, loyal friend, faithful husband, and protective father. Why would someone want to murder me? For what? The investigation began within days. Soon becoming a high profile case with a lot of people watching each other.

I knew the police around Blairsville, Indiana County, and the Indiana State Police would be tripping over one another. The old saying goes . . . two's a pair and three's a crowd. With Trooper Kevin Foley a member of the Indiana State Police crime investigative unit . . . you can see the direction in which my murder case is headed. Who's going to try to prove it? The Fraternal Order of Police? It will be a power struggle all the way so I can only be optimistic that Chief Hess of the Blairsville Police Department will be able to maintain his status as lead investigator. Is he capable? He's been in law enforcement for thirty years give or take a few, so I would consider him to be a seasoned lawmen. The ball is in his court.

Authors note: As a researcher I am convinced that the Dr. John Yelenic Story will one day become a textbook case in victimology. If only someone was willing to follow the case to the VERY end. Not stopping when the trial is over like so many books and television shows do. This story goes beyond the conviction, carting the guilty away to jail while waiting for all the appeals to be exhausted. This tale has legs. There is more to come . . . just wait!

CHAPTER EIGHT

*Secrets that are heavy to bear we keep from
the ears of those who are too near.*

Sandwiched between Cpl. Janelle Lydic of the Blairsville Police Department and Indiana County Coroner Mike Baker, Chief Hess gave his first news conference to the media. He delivered the very basic details of Dr. John Yelenic's murder or as much as he was able to disclose to the public without causing a panic with a killer still on the loose. He stated that they had been questioning Yelenic's neighbors, searching inside and outside of his house for leads. However, if anything Chief Hess did state that the victim was *targeted*. He knew that fact as far back as 2001. Michele would call him to have John arrested or have a PFA documented or for whatever reason she could come up at the time. In other words, *targeted* rolled right off his tongue. I think he probably knew all along that one day the death of Dr. John Yelenic would be on his door step.

Just two weeks prior, John woke up to find his car spray painted and called the police department to report it. They never found out who did it. Nor did it cross anyone's mind that that incident could have been either a ploy for his killer to test the local law enforcement or, on a personal level to John, a preview of what was to come. Months prior to that spray painting incident John had his attorney open a fund to hire a private investigator to prove that Michele Yelenic and Kevin Foley had their hands in his demise. John had no other enemies after him to his knowledge. Effie also persuaded his cousin Mary Ann to become executrix of his estate. That way Mary Ann could keep a close eye on his finances, making sure JJ would become beneficiary of all funds available to him at the age of eighteen. His intentions, like any father, would be to care for his child. It was stated repeatedly by John's friends and family that John always felt guilty because Michele (being the mother even if a child is adopted) had **MORE** of a legal right to care for JJ than he had as the adoptive father. It wasn't fair. When he was able to get back in control of the divorce agreement and going forward . . . look where it got him.

Michele had to realize if John went for full custody of JJ down the road, her meal ticket would be permanently gone. Which could be why John's life was doomed. Even if the cost was Trooper Kevin Foley, who just happened to be a willing player in the plan. Everyone is disposable to a person who has little or no conscience. Foley's own hatred kept him from using basic logic. Boy what a sucker he was. Michele always knows how to get what she wants . . . she's a pro at it. Remember, she's been used to entitlements her entire life. Her children represent monthly support checks from their fathers. "And just keep the checks coming," is what her brother John Magyar quoted her as saying. Who would want to believe such a thing when he was in love with Michele? Love is blind. Dr. John Yelenic paid the ultimate price with his life. Who's looking out for JJ now?

The one question on everyone's mind early in the investigations was why Michele and Trooper Foley weren't called in for questioning that afternoon or early evening on April 13, 2006? Officer Jill Gaston of the Blairsville police did go to Michele's home to report the death that evening between the hours of 9:30 p.m. and 11:00 p.m. Kevin had reported to the Indiana barracks that morning at 8:00 a.m. and worked an entire shift just like any other day. Remember, Yelenic's body was not discovered *that* afternoon until 3:30 p.m. Why couldn't Chief Hess have called an Indiana judge early the evening of April 13th to obtain a warrant? He could have had them both brought directly to the Blairsville police station for questioning. The cut above Kevin's eye could have still been swabbed. Perhaps some trace of Yelenic's DNA may have remained under the skin tissue. If anything, this action would have made Foley feel as if he was definitely "a person of interest." Officer Gaston stated under oath that she noticed a *fresh cut* above Foley's left eye the night she went to Michele's home (April 13th) to report on the death of Michele's husband, Dr. Yelenic. Surely all Foley's co-workers couldn't help but notice a bright red cut above his eye that morning. He claimed the injury happened after hockey practice the evening of April 12th. While placing his stick into the rear of his SUV, it clipped his forehead just above his eye. I don't think everyone was buying that excuse. Especially when word got out that a dentist in Blairsville was murdered in his home around the time practice had ended in Delmont (with additional travel time factored in to reach Blairsville). Surveillance cameras located at various businesses along the route traced a SUV Ford Explorer traveling toward Blairsville at 12:19 a.m. (there about) on the early morning of April 13, 2006.

Since Cpl. Lydic answered the 911 call of April 13, 2006, she maintained the role of lead investigator of the homicide. She contacted Mary Ann for the names and phone numbers of Dr. Yelenic's friends and family members. She returned to the murder scene to retrieve additional evidence such as John's address book, photos and personal papers found in the living room, dining room, and upstairs bedroom. The bloody shoeprints left behind by the killer had everyone's interest. The print was unique! Because the victim's body was found bare footed, the print had to be that of the killer. The size was estimated to be 10 or 10 1/2. With crime scene investigators and analysis the style and brand was determined to be a sport running shoe. So now they had to find the owner.

As the weeks wore on, investigators seized bank accounts, interviewed people John had lent money to in the past, any sexual encounters he had, and activities in his dental practice among the employees. Everyone must have felt as if they were under the magnifying glass. Cpl. Lydic worked on those leads for months. John Yelenic's life was like a open book. Surely some of the information may have shocked those closest to him. If anything, Cpl. Lydic's business skills were excellent. She was able to compile a massive binder about three and a half inches thick complete with crime scene logs, photos of every "person of interest" she had interviewed, along with their statements.

Back in July of 2008, I interviewed Cpl. Lydic at Mary Ann Clark's home. She held the binder close to her body as she sat on the couch, telling us of all the sections and materials she had accumulated from April 13, 2006, to the present. According to Cpl. Lydic there were several copies. She kept one at her disposal at all times, just in case she was called upon to locate a piece of incriminating information. There were even updated ones compiled. Plus a box or two of folders filled with crime reports, logs, interviews by other law enforcement agencies, crime scene investigations, and photos, to name a few. All of which sat in the Blairsville police station's evidence room. Remember, you'll only learn the information THEY want you to ascertain. Control is everything, stated an officer to me once and boy was he correct.

The most active role by the Blairsville Police Department was taken from April through June 2006. By the end of June, Indiana's District Attorney Robert (Bob) Bell persisted in the attempt to dominate the murder case of Dr. John Yelenic. What really made him decide right then and why? One reason could have been because Mary Ann and John's friends Tim Abbey and Dennis Vaughn were pushing the envelope harder for the need to call the Attorney General's Office of Pennsylvania for assistance. Keep in mind, D.A. Bell had to address the Indiana State Police command in his county of Indiana while they were trying to do their best to keep the lid on the case and the media out. The last thing D.A. Bell needed was to get Tom Corbett, the Attorney General aboard. His involvement would automatically open the doors to a full fledged investigation by sending in his own agents and legal team to begin a *non biases* probe.

That's exactly what transpired by July 2006. Now the Blairsville Police, Indiana County, Indiana State Police,

Greensburg State Police (lab), Allegheny County homicide detectives, and the FBI out of the Pittsburgh field office began an all-out investigation. This meant six law enforcement agencies were involved in reviewing, analyzing, and re-examining every detail in the murder case of Dr. John Yelenic. One would think a serial killer was on the loose with this much law enforcement swarming around.

When it comes down to one of their own entangled in such a mess, handling internal matters becomes a slippery slope. Let's not forget the most incriminating clues left behind. The DNA found underneath the victim's fingernails and those bloody running shoeprints on the floors throughout the hallways and rooms on the first floor of the victim's home. Those were two pieces of evidence left behind by the assailant that couldn't be denied. Moreover, they became crucial in supportive evidence which brought the case to court on March 9, 2009. Even though neither the knife, the shoes nor the bloody clothing the assailant wore during the killing have been found to this day. Which is why, even now, this act of **death needs answers.**

CHAPTER NINE

*The definition of a friend is one attached
to another by feelings of personal regard.*

As Dennis Vaughn explains . . .

John was one of those individuals whose life seemed to be marked by more than his fair share of difficulties and trauma, starting almost from birth. While we were all horrified by the events that led to his death, I think it is fair to say that none of us who were close to John were particularly shocked. We had all watched his life being slowly taken from him in recent years, leaving him a veritable shell of the vibrant and outgoing man we all knew and loved. Could we have done more to help him? Could we have foreseen the tragedy of April 13, 2006 and intervened in such a way as to help John avoid his violent end? These questions will haunt John's survivors for years to come, maybe forever. However, none of these questions will ever have the emotional impact of *Why*? Why did John have to be taken from us? Who could have hated this kind and generous person so much that they could not bear to have him alive? What kind of world is it where the desire for money, material goods or power would supersede the basic honoring of another human being's existence?

It would be a lofty goal indeed to try to answer these questions within the confines of this book. There are limits to our ability to understand the motives of others and to make sense of a senseless world. I have provided therapy and counseling to individuals of all ages and walks of life over the years, yet I would venture to say that my understanding of the human condition is no better than anyone's. In fact, the more I delve into the case of John's murder and the motivations that led to it, the more I realize that my understanding of human nature may be less than average. I do not know how a person can reach a point in their lives where their material desires become an all-consuming passion, where they care not who they must hurt to get where they wish to be. Shakespeare, Poe, Hemingway, Capote—among other great writers—have all tried to peer into the darkness of the human heart, trying to lay bare what is so often hidden. Yet, here we are still seeking answers. All we can do is continue the search with the hope of someday understanding.

John's story needs to be told. For the most part, he suffered the last few years of his life in relative silence, not sharing the deepest and darkest of his secret pain, even with those who were his closest confidants. In many ways, I believe that his silence provided assistance to the evil forces that were conspiring to rob him of his happiness, his livelihood, and ultimately, his life. He will be silent no more. Through this writing, and through the words of many others who had the honor and pleasure of being in

John's inner circle, his story will finally be told. It is the least I can do for the man who was the closest thing to a brother I have ever had.

I packed my bags in the fall of '85 and made my way to Juniata College for my freshman year. That is when I first met John Yelenic. Nestled in the mountains of rural central Pennsylvania, Juniata is a small, liberal arts college that maintains a student body of about 1300 students. About 30 miles south of State College, home of the massive Penn State University, it was a sleepy little school in a sleepy little town.

Juniata had, and still maintains, a reputation as being an excellent school for science, particularly biology and chemistry. This reputation, coupled with the comfortable school environment and the extraordinarily high faculty-to-student ratio, attracted many recruits who wished to major in pre-medicine, pre-dentistry, biology, or chemistry. I was among this group, as I wanted to go on to a career in medicine and believed that Juniata was my best ticket to that destination.

As is typical, the first person I met at Juniata was my roommate, a young man from eastern Pennsylvania named Steve. Unlike me, Steve came to Juniata with the benefit of having friends from high school who also came to the college. His two high school friends lived in the all-male dorm across the campus courtyard, and it was not long before I met them through Steve. One of his friends, Rob, had a roommate named Eric that I began to hang around with. Being more sociable than me, Eric introduced me to his other freshman friends from the dorm. Little did I know at the time that one end of a dormitory hallway would eventually provide me with the closest friends I have ever known in my life. John Yelenic was among that number, as well as Tim Abbey, Dave

Lavrich, Mark Woomer, Scott Kelley, and Dan Ressler. To this day, I have never known such deep friendships and, I firmly believe, I never will again in this lifetime.

There was no doubt that, even out of this collection of guys, John was unique. People were drawn to him from the first time they met him. The thing that people noticed first about him was his sense of humor. His loud belly-laugh and his knack of brashly saying whatever was on his mind caused him to stand out clearly from the crowd. You could be sure that if there was laughter on that hall, John was somehow involved. Beneath the humor, though, there was a kindness and a caring for others that was obvious.

John and I shared many classes together during our years at Juniata. One of my most vivid memories was being his laboratory partner in a microbiology course. The semester was spent growing molds, spores, and bacteria in Petrie dishes. Literally, we spent time watching mold grow, as boring as that sounds. However, John found a way to make this activity fun. That became a pattern in my relationship with John. No matter how unpleasant the activity, John could bring humor to it and make it bearable. This was still true at his funeral 21 years later. The evening after John was laid to rest, a large group of John's friends gathered to reminisce about our time with John. Tears of sorrow that had just begun to dry on our faces quickly turned to tears of laughter as we regaled each other with "John stories," each more outrageous than the next.

After college, our career plans necessitated that we go in different directions. Many of us had plans for graduate school. John went to the University of Pittsburgh Dental School, still adhering to his master plan. I left for Edinboro University, near Erie, PA, to pursue a master's degree in clinical psychology. We tried to have contact as much as we could, but the demands of our lives were making it more and more difficult. After graduate school, the members of our circle of friends began to get married. First Scott, then Tim, then myself. Although phone contact was maintained, we never got to see as much of each other in person during those years as we would have liked. As my life progressed into a full-time career as a therapist, as well as a father, I did not hear much from John. It was during this time, though, that he met Michele and began his ill-fated relationship with her. The first time I met Michele was at a party held at my home in Bradford, PA. My parents were in attendance as well and I vividly remember my father pulling me aside and, saying of Michele whom he had just met, "John better watch this one." When I asked what he meant, he said he had a bad feeling about her and that maybe she was after John's money. I did not believe him, which is only proof that my father's years of life experience made him much wiser than I was. He saw something in one brief contact with Michele that so many of us missed. If only we could have seen it too and convinced John to see it as well.

After a bad experience with my local dentist in Bradford, I decided that I would see John for my dental needs. Not only would I be treated by a great dentist, it would also give me an excuse to go visit him a couple of times a year for cleanings, checkups, etc. It was during one of these visits, after he had been married to Michele for some time, that he told me of their plans to adopt a child from Russia. He and Michele showed me a heart-breaking video of an orphanage in Russia where infants were laid out on a wooden table with raised sides. They looked, for all the world, like puppies on display in a pet shop. John told me how the children often laid so long without being turned over that they would develop flat spots in their skulls. This was not due to negligence of the orphanages, per se, but rather because there were so many orphans and too few staff to give them the individual attention that they needed.

I knew that John and Michele had been trying to conceive for some time. They had difficulties with this process, with John eventually undergoing testing. John, never the one to be shy about personal issues, toasted loudly to his elevated sperm count one night in a crowded bar in State College, PA. He was plenty fertile. They then began an expensive series of fertilization treatments for Michele, often requiring John to give her injections of medications. Little did anyone other than Michele know that she had had her tubes tied years earlier. No fertilization treatments were ever going to be successful under those circumstances. To this day, I have no idea why she would have John spend so much money on useless treatments. My suspicion, though, is that she may have wanted a child without having to wreck her body through pregnancy. She may have fooled John, who desperately wanted a child, that she was barren and, therefore, adoption was the only option. Yet another tragedy in this story is that John went to his grave cheated out of the joy of creating a child of his own.

By the spring of 2002, John's marriage to Michele had started to unravel at a rapid rate. He left their expansive home in Indiana and moved to a modest house in Blairsville that he owned as a rental property. John, generous even during difficult times, agreed to let the family who was renting the home stay there for a few months until they could find other housing. As he told me, he did not have the heart to dislocate children on such short notice. In the interim, John lived in a trailer that was owned by an associate that he knew from a lab that manufactured dentures for his practice.

My own marriage was coming to an end in the fall of 2002. John was my closest confidante during that period of my life. He came all the way down to Virginia, where I was living at that point, to help me pack my things and move out of my home. This was an extremely low point in my life as I packed my belongings, leaving behind a 5 year old son and a two year old daughter that were the centers of my universe. John, who hated to see anyone in pain which is ironic considering his career choice, cajoled me into going to the movies with him that night to cheer me up. The movie *Jackass* had just come out. I told him I was not in the mood but he insisted. In spite of myself and the state I was in, I could not help laughing during the movie. I was not laughing at the movie as much as I was at John, himself. His belly-laugh drowned out the film's dialogue at times and I could not help but smile and laugh, even with the pain. I count this among the many other debts that I owe John that I will never be able to repay.

Also that weekend, John told me that our friend Dave Lavrich had assisted John in moving out of his home when he separated from Michele. He informed me that Dave helped him and now he helped me. Therefore, it was now my turn in the rotation and that I was the one who would have to help the next in our circle of friends if/when they got divorced. Unfortunately, I served my turn a few years later when Tim separated from his wife. Tim, you are on the hook now, my friend.

John and I became closer than ever following our respective separations. We spent countless weekends visiting each other, with either me going to Blairsville or him coming to Virginia. While I loved having the ability to hang out with John more than I had in years, it was bittersweet. It was during this time that John was embroiled in his divorce and custody battles with Michele. John, who had been so robust and larger-than-life, now began to deteriorate before my very eyes. Over the next few years, I watched him take to drinking more and more and gaining weight. He also began to suffer the signs of depression, including sleeplessness and moodiness. He was not the same person that he was in college. The war with Michele was taking its toll. Being accused of physical abuse, accused of sexual abuse, being taken from his office in handcuffs and made to sit in a jail cell, and being denied access to his son were like individual nails in his slow but methodical crucifixion.

When Michele became involved with Kevin Foley, John became scared. He knew that Michele would only become involved with someone who was not wealthy if there was something in it for her. Having a close ally in law enforcement would allow Michele to escalate her trumped-up charges against John. When the intimidation and threats against John began to ratchet up, he started to come visit me more frequently in Virginia than I came to see him. This was his preference, he said. He stated that he felt a certain relief when he crossed the Mason-Dixon Line because he knew he was safely away from everything at home. Sadly, John had lived the majority of his life in Blairsville, the sleepy little town that was dear to his heart, but now he couldn't even feel comfortable there.

At the end of January 2005, I began dating Lisa, who has since become my wife. Several weeks later, I took Lisa on a weekend trip to Blairsville to meet my best friend. We drove north in a blinding snowstorm as I tried my best to describe John and to share stories of the adventures that we had. I think I talked during the entire 3 hour trip and probably still did not scratch the surface. It did not take long, though, for Lisa and John to become friends. Some people might be shy or even standoffish when meeting their friend's new girlfriend for the first time, but this was not in John's character make-up. He welcomed her as if he knew her for years. It did not take long for Lisa to begin to feel comfortable, even in this stranger's house so far from her home.

   I had just picked my children up to spend the Easter weekend at my home when I received the phone call that John had died. John's neighbor Susan called me and I immediately knew something was horribly wrong before I even began to understand the words she was speaking. Usually a very upbeat person, Susan was choking back tears as she tried to form the words "John is dead." I must not have heard her correctly, I thought, and asked her to repeat. She told me that John was dead. Apparently, John had been found dead and there was a front window broken at his house. Immediately, I thought of the windows that were directly behind his living room couch. *My God*, I thought, *John shot himself*. I could envision John taking one of his handguns, putting it under his chin, and pulling the trigger in his front room, finally having reached the point of exhaustion from his years of battling Michele. I could imagine the bullet tearing through his skull and shattering the window behind him. *Why did I not see this coming? I assess people for suicide risk for a living and had just seen him a few days ago. Could I have missed the signs*, I thought. If so, I would never be able to live with myself.

   I immediately turned the car around and called my ex-wife, telling her that I needed to bring the children home immediately. Not wanting to upset the kids, I just told her that something was wrong with John. Both of my kids knew John, and loved him like an uncle. I then called Lisa and then my parents. I then made the call I dreaded most, calling our friend Tim. Tim is easily the most emotional of my friends, which is usually a positive thing. However, I also knew that Tim would take John's death extremely hard and probably blame himself for not doing more to protect John from this fate.

After promising my children that we would re-schedule our weekend and that I would make it up to them, I made the long drive home, my mind racing. My phone continued to ring as more details began to trickle in. There were rumors that John suffered a heart attack. This was not a huge shock considering the stress he had been under and how he had neglected his health over the past couple of years. I then received a call that confirmed that John was dead and that it was being investigated as a homicide. My blood ran cold at the mention of that word and my immediate thought was "Foley."

Foley and Michele had been harassing John for some time and John knew that Foley hated him intensely. In fact, outside of Foley and Michele, I could not think of a single person that disliked him, let alone hated him enough to snuff out his life. When I later heard that there were no signs of robbery, I became absolutely convinced that Foley and, possibly, Michele were behind this heinous act.

The visitation was surreal. I could not bring myself to believe that the lifeless corpse in the funeral home was my best friend. He wore a black turtleneck to cover the horrific neck wounds that he suffered. The best mortician in the world could not have made those wounds presentable. In all the years I knew him, I had never known John to wear a turtleneck, which only added further to my sense of unreality. John's family, friends, and acquaintances clung to each other, in a state of deep emotional shock. Each person I spoke to was in agreement that Foley was the prime suspect in this. We all knew of John's ongoing struggles with his estranged wife and her state trooper boyfriend.

Following the funeral, Lisa and I went directly to the Blairsville Police Department to give our statements to investigators as we had visited John only a few days before the murder. Lisa and I both answered the questions posed to us in individual interviews and both stated our belief that Foley needed to be brought in for questioning. We were horrified that a couple of days after the murder, Foley still had not been questioned. *How could I be questioned before Foley?*, I thought.

As I left the police station, a reporter from Geraldo Rivera's syndicated news program caught me and asked if she could speak to me on camera. I answered her questions as politically as I could, but I desperately wanted to proclaim as loudly as I could who I believed was responsible for this atrocity. Apparently, someone told her about Michele and Foley because when the segment finally aired, it showed her attempting to get an interview from Michele and being turned away at the door. Michele did not come to the visitation or to the funeral. Now she was not talking to police or to reporters. Were we the only ones who could see just how suspicious all this looked?

I truly believed that an arrest was imminent. The crime scene was a bloody mess, with footprints all over. Surely, there must be forensic evidence that would allow the case to be solved. Each day I waited for the phone call that Foley had been arrested. Days turned to weeks, weeks turned to months, and before we knew it 2006 was over and we were well into 2007. We had heard that Foley had been placed on administrative duty with the State Police. It didn't seem like much of a punishment to me. Instead of risking his life to uphold the law like other state troopers do every day, he was sitting safely behind a desk somewhere. He also was able to spend time with his children on a daily basis for all those months. Of course, he also was able to spend each day with Michele, so maybe there was a bit of punishment after all.

CHAPTER TEN

If there is a shadow of a doubt . . .
why count on it?

The local Blairsville police and Indiana County investigators were focused on John Yelenic's next door neighbors Tom and Melissa Uss. They were classified as "persons of interest" early on in the investigation. Throughout 2006 the Uss's were interviewed over and over again. Then they were even separated in the attempt to see if one of them would slip up under questioning and give law enforcement enough motive to justify arresting one of them for the murder of Dr. John Yelenic. Their lives were changed forever by all the speculative rumors that spread throughout Blairsville like wild fire.

Tom and Melissa still had to go to work every day, keep up with Craig and Zak's school activities, attend church and take care of Melissa's ailing mother. They were under tremendous strain day in and day out, while trying to comprehend how their high school friend could have been murdered within earshot of their home. They knew all the trouble John's estranged wife had put him through over the years—her lifestyle, numerous divorce issues over property, money and, most importantly, visitation arrangements concerning JJ. Who could possibly be behind such a horrific murder? One person's name immediately came to mind. But how could they prove it?

At this point I would like to give the reader background details about Tom and Melissa Uss. Tom was two years older than John. They met during high school and maintained a solid friendship through the years. Melissa was a few years younger and worked with John on the yearbook committee and both were members of the Blairsville High School marching band. Upon graduation Tom enlisted in the United States Navy, John enrolled in college and Melissa did secretarial work for several businesses in town. The Uss's married in the mid- 1980s. Melissa accompanied Tom while he was on active duty. After receiving an honorable discharge, Tom retired from the Navy in February 2006. They decided to return to their hometown of Blairsville. On a prior visit they were shown several homes that were for sale, finally deciding the home at 227 S. Spring Street was perfect. Their sons, Craig and Zak, would have their own bedrooms and a large backyard to play. Melissa and the boys moved in prior to Tom's retirement date so the boys could begin the school year without any disruptions.

After establishing his dental practice by mid-1995, John decided to move out of his mother's home and purchase his own home just a few blocks from her. He moved into 233 S. Spring Street, next door to his high school friends Tom and Melissa. John was just two blocks away from his dental practice on Market Street, too. Everything appeared to be working out just fine for all of them.

When Michele, Nicole, and Nathan moved in with John during the summer of 1997 (after the passing of his mother), the children quickly made friends with the neighborhood children. However, Michele didn't appear to be that taken with the area nor the neighbors. By this time, John had purchased a two-karat engagement ring for her. According to her brother John Magyar's interview, Michele couldn't wait to flaunt her diamond in front of the gals at the welfare office. She had graduated from welfare to wealth. In no time, her newly established status fueled her growing dissatisfaction with residing in Blairsville, and she looked to relocate the family. What better place than her old stomping grounds of Indiana, Pennsylvania (about twenty-five miles northeast)? John's successful dental practice encouraged them to focus on a more upscale neighborhood. While they looked, John rented out his house so it wouldn't sit vacant. The marriage between John Yelenic and Michele Magyar-Kamler took place December 1997 in Las Vegas, rounding out the year . . . and what a year it was.

A re-cap . . . Mary Lois dies, John makes Michele the beneficiary of his will in June (they weren't even married), then marries Michele in December while packing up to move out of his house in Blairsville. Tom, Melissa, Craig, and Zak continued to see John as their family dentist throughout the years, as well as attending Badger hockey games in which Nathan and Craig played.

All things, both good and bad, come to an end. John's life in Indiana began to fall apart as his legal separation from Michele materialized in 2002, after four frustrating years of marriage. Many of John's close friends and family would agree that it never qualified as a marriage in the first place. Michele stopped having a relationship with John shortly after they adopted JJ from Russia in 2001. Michele's image as a warm and loving mother began to fade away as she resorted to her old lifestyle. She announced her engagement (while still married to John) and insisted that he move out of the White Farm home in Indiana. Since his home in Blairsville was occupied, he rented a trailer until his tenants' lease ended. Once they moved out, he contacted his cousin Tracy Jacobs to come over and make several improvements and paint the interior.

Michele also moved to Johnstown with Nicole, Nathan, and JJ. They lived in her new fiancé S. Glosser's home until their engagement was broken off in 2003. Right when Michele might have been counting her lucky stars, Glosser's mother brought her down to earth by insisting that Michele sign a pre-nuptial agreement before any thoughts of a marriage took place. Mother Glosser was securing family assets that had been in the family for generations. Packing up their belongings, Michele and the kids made their way back to Indiana

The fireworks began again as Michele constantly called John's home and dental practice, insisting that he purchase another home for their son JJ to live in or they would be homeless. How would it look if a dentist making $300,000.00 a year had his son living in the streets? Of course, she insisted that the home had to be in another upscale area of Indiana, a condition upon which John agreed to keep peace and make the children happy.

Back on Spring Street, the neighborhood came alive again as John pulled his car up to the curb in front of his three-story yellow-brick house. The kids on the block came running up to his car to help him unload boxes and suitcases. All of them liked John, who treated them to pizza parties and allowed them to borrow his video games. He even designed a weight room in the basement, equipped with bench presses, punching bag and a stationary bicycle. When Craig and Nathan visited, they were always welcome to work out. Melissa and Tom would have weekly barbecues, inviting John, their families, and friends, and the kids on the block. A small plastic swimming pool was filled with water for JJ, Zak, and the other young children.

Melissa enjoyed cooking and baking for the group which brought back their shared memories of happy times growing up in a small town. Breads, pastries, and cakes were her specialties. For years Melissa's closest friends encouraged her to open a bakery. By February of 2006, she and Tom decided to apply for a small business loan. After sitting down with the loan officer at their local bank, they were able to develop a business plan. As the weeks passed, they were informed that more funding would be necessary for the down payment. Even with the loan and additional financial assistance from Melissa's family they would still need an additional $15, 000.00. John, aware of their disappointment, offered a personal loan in the amount needed to finalize the contract. He supported Tom and Melissa's bakery one hundred percent. After all, their friendship had existed over twenty years. To John they were like family. The Uss's insisted on paying the loan back as soon as they could, but John was just happy to lend a helping hand. Knowing that the bakery was a long time dream of theirs, he wished his friends success.

As fate would have it, a turn of events took place at the end of March 2006. While John was negotiating his divorce agreement with Attorney Alexander, out of nowhere came a bomb shell. Due to the division of assets agreement, Michele had received additional income of about $100,000 during 2005. She decided to file her own taxes declaring she was single, and claim Nicole, Nathan and JJ as her dependents. Wait a minute. The divorce hadn't been filed yet, let alone processed! Having claimed all four as deductions in past years, John realized that this maneuver created a financial disaster for him. How could he come up with the amount needed to pay his taxes and fast?

He had to ask Tom and Melissa to return the $15,000.00 loan, but assured them that he would replace the full amount by the end of April. On April 7, 2006 a $15,000.00 check was made payable to John Yelenic and returned to him by Melissa and Tom.

Law enforcement agencies soon focused on *the check*. According to them it had to be the motive they needed to build a suspicious case as to why Dr. John Yelenic was murdered. The check kept the Uss's under the magnifying glass for over a year. Throughout the ranks of the Blairsville Police Department, Indiana County Police, Indiana State Police, and the Greensburg State Police doubts abounded.

Feeling as if the walls were closing in, Melissa welcomed the invitation from her mother and a group of her friends and attended a luncheon at a bed and breakfast in Indiana. Sister psychics Suzanne Kelley and Jean Vincent provided readings. As Melissa's mother was being read, John Yelenic's spirit was felt by Suzanne. Surprised at all the details surrounding the circumstances of John's murder that Suzanne offered during the reading, Melissa asked if Suzanne and Jean would like to go to John's home where the crime took place to see if more insights would come forth. They agreed to further assist. Melissa wanted to see if John's family would consent to the idea and she contacted Mary Ann who welcomed any leads to the murder of her cousin.

July 8, 2006 was the first time the two psychics entered Dr. John Yelenic's home with Melissa. More information was channeled through Suzanne and Jean telling of the details leading up to the murder, such as how John was murdered, why he was murdered, who was present, what was left behind and so on. Melissa decided to contact Corporal Lydic, the lead investigator of the Yelenic case, about the informative details just revealed. Another gathering at 233 S. Spring Street followed on July 24, 2006. This time, in addition to Melissa, Suzanne, and Jean, Corporal Lydic, District Attorney Bob Bell of Indiana County and one of his detectives attended.

The psychics disclosed other possibilities to the lawmen that hot afternoon in July, even offering the possibility that one of their own might have committed the crime! Law enforcement in the area can't afford that kind of negative image getting out to the media. That would only accelerate intense public interest just when police were hoping they had their man with the next door neighbor being their prime suspect. A simple open and close case for them. Now this information. When this news got back to the Indiana State Police barracks they had something to ponder. The doubts were now surfacing which had to make law enforcement at all levels extremely uncomfortable over the months that followed. If Melissa's objective was to take the intense heat off her and her family, I think she accomplished it.

Going into the winter months of 2007 (just after the arrest of Trooper Kevin Foley on September 27, 2007), I wanted to keep the case alive in the public eye, so I contacted Mary Ann suggesting we arrange to have Suzanne and Jean come to John's house to do a re-enactment—just like they did back in July of 2006 for District Attorney Bell—to see if they could provide us with any further insights into the murder. She agreed and everyone arrived on November 15, 2007 about 1:00 p.m. I filmed and documented the session. Local television Channel 4 wanted to offer it live to their viewers during the five and six o'clock news reports. Jennifer Miele, her cameraman, the *Tribune Review* newspaper reporter Paul Pierce, Melissa Uss, Mary Ann Clark, and myself were present as the psychics prepared to set the mood.

This section is from my film:

Channel 4 reporter Jennifer Miele and her camera man filmed an introduction and conclusion segment as well as a few shots of the psychics and Melissa together talking as she reported the story.

JEAN: Opened with who attended the walk through in July which were D.A. Bob Bell, Dave, and Cpl. Lydic.

D.A. Bob Bell asked Jean if she thinks it will be solved? The truth . . . it will. It may take time however, justice will prevail. However, not on HIS watch. (He was to be up for re-election in 2008). She stated it was the 'Good Old Boys Club' involved.

People involved in a cover up scheme.

Law enforcement. Even as unthinkable as it may seem. It is.

At that moment, Dave (the detective from Indiana County) stated that the murder had to be done by someone in the Navy. Which of course was aimed toward Melissa's husband Tom.

However, it was on the tip of his tongue. They were indeed fixated on the next door neighbor Tom Uss from the get go.

Symbolism was explained by Jean that becomes apparent in a crime scene. Being present in the same state that the crime was committed in pieces of the event comes forth like film clips. She could feel John fighting for his life. The blood around her feet. The points she demonstrated across her chest as to where impact took place from a sharp object (knife).

SUE: Stated the knife was like a box cutter. Thin and very sharp. The assailant wore a necklace similar to an Italian horn. Dave reached under his collar and pulled out a chain with an Italian horn stating all the brothers of Indiana wear one. She then stated that there would be no fingerprints found in the house other than John's. However, John did scratch his assailant. Something was left behind. It has to be examined by experts. She was sure it was facial. The intruder came in from the kitchen door. The tree house is where he sat waiting and watching John.

JEAN: There were two vehicles near the house in the back. One root beer color SUV. The other was a gold car. A female was present. Very cold hearted, negative. "Let's go, let's go . . . is he dead yet?"

As Jean snapped her fingers she had everyone's undivided attention for the moment. Therefore, there were 2 males and 1 female at the house. It was a plan, she added.

SUE: Differed, sensing just 2 males present. This case will be solved as the AG (Attorney General's) office gathers more evidence. Mentioned clothes worn by killer was burned.

JEAN: Had given Melissa the location which was near a large silo. Melissa visited the spot and sure enough there was an area where the ground was destroyed as if a fire had taken place there. She had even taken a phone picture of it and sent it on to Jean. When Jean mentioned it to the Indiana County police back in July 2006, they suggested she and Sue take them to the spot. No way were they going to enter into such a situation like that so she just gave them the location to go on their own to investigate. However, to Melissa's surprise it was still undisturbed when she saw it back then.

As the walkthrough ended, Jennifer Miele closed the segment stating clues were given to the police to investigate such as the DNA under John Yelenic's nails, type of knife, and bloody footprints found on the floor of the dining room.

Re-cap: The DNA did prove to be from Trooper Kevin Foley. The bloody footprints came from the shoes Foley wore. Which remained on the dining room floor until 2009 after the conviction of Foley. The clothes and knife have not been found to date.

On November 16, 2007 Paul Pierce's article appeared in the *Tribune Review* (Westmoreland) section of this event.

CHAPTER ELEVEN

Trying our best to make goodness attractive can be one of the toughest assignments to claim.

A Grand Jury convened in the Federal Building on Grant Street in downtown Pittsburgh the second week of May 2007. Some eighty subpoenas had been issued to those individuals who had personal dealings with John Yelenic within the past ten years. As the witnesses testified, further crucial details were exposed. Michele Magyar-Kamler-Yelenic was subpoenaed. It was the *first* and *last* time she took the witness stand in her husband's murder trial.

It didn't take long for the Grand Jury to reach their decision. Much of the damaging details came from Foley's co-workers who stated that he had been seen flipping his knife in and out, cleaning his fingernails with it, stabbing other officers in the groin, and so forth. After the murder of John Yelenic, however, no one ever saw Trooper Foley with his knife again. I'm not sure if the DNA results had been finalized at that point. Nowhere did I find that information documented for the public knowledge. By July 2007 a charge of homicide was established. That meant that motive and opportunity had been confirmed. Eyes were now fixed on PA State Trooper Kevin Foley, badge # 5770.

Shortly after April 2006, Foley was transferred to the State Police Barracks in Hollidaysburg, PA, about thirty-five miles east of Indiana, PA. His "new job" was to issue uniforms to troopers. Pretty much what I would call a desk job, especially since he had to surrender his gun. Foley had to have known he was under suspicion, if not the number one suspect. However, for eighteen months Foley lived in a nice house, had Michele and the children around him so he could play "father," was able to attend hockey games, eat out at restaurants, go to a movie, run races, and socialize with friends. Living a carefree life while family members and friends of the victim were coping with their loss and trying every day to seek justice so no one would forget the price Dr. Yelenic paid for whatever life he had during the weeks and months leading up to his murder. But, as we all have learned growing up, all good things eventually come to an end. In Foley's case it was coming to a screeching halt unexpectedly.

Out of the blue, on the morning of September 27, 2007, he was called into the office by his supervisor at the Hollidaysburg Barrack and to his SURPRISE . . . he was handcuffed while his Miranda rights were read to him by one of his own! How sweet can that be? Escorted out to an awaiting State Police vehicle, he was transferred to the Indiana County Jail, fingerprinted, photographed and placed in a cell. He then had to wait for his preliminary hearing to take place within six weeks.

Upon Foley's arrest on September 27th, PA Attorney General Tom Corbett held a press conference, attended by all law enforcement agencies in the area of Indiana County and the local news media, to announce the arrest of Trooper Foley for the murder of Dr. John Yelenic. I attended the conference and filmed Attorney General Corbett reading from the Grand Jury findings. I could see the relief on the faces of Mary Ann and her husband Dave when that leg of the journey was reached. Finally there was going to be justice for John Yelenic.

On November 9, 2007 at 8:30 a.m. at the magistrates' office (next to the courthouse), Indiana District Judge Guy Harberl was confronted with a standing room only courtroom. There were probably more law enforcement personnel inside than on the streets of Indiana during the hearing. Kevin Foley was represented by a defense team headed by Attorney Thomas Johnson of Indiana and, as second chair, Attorney Richard Galloway of Greensburg. The prosecution was assigned to Senior Deputy Attorney General Anthony Krastek. The local, county, and state police knew Attorney Johnson quite well because he defended locally arrested offenders at the Indiana Courthouse. Attorney Galloway was from the same mold, but his practice was based in Greensburg in Westmoreland County. Both were seasoned defense attorneys, which may have given Foley some sense of hope early on.

Attorney Galloway's style came across as smooth and confident. He attached his defense to each and every detail. Nothing got by him. Like a bull dog biting onto a shoe and not letting go. Creating doubt was his specialty. On the other hand, Attorney Krastek's style was one of command, direct, aggressive when he had to be, and confident at all times. His dramatics and animated body language kept the jury and audience alert at all times, especially during the sidebar discussions.

During the entire hearing, Foley simply sat staring straight ahead at Judge Harberl. He didn't react to any of the bloody photos of Yelenic when they were displayed to the right of him on a flat-screen television. Every once in a while Attorney Galloway would reach over and show Foley a piece of paper. Who knew what the message was. Maybe words like "relax" or "breathe"! Only once did Foley make eye contact with one of his colleagues while he was on the witness stand. It was simply a glance. There were the "no shows" of course: Michele, Nicole, and Nathan. They might have been too scared to go anywhere near the courthouse for fear they would be arrested, too. Members of the media were there doing their job, interviewing anyone and everyone connected to the case. This had to be the biggest event in Indiana since the days of Jimmy Stewart.

Inside the courtroom as the hearing progressed, Atty. Galloway maintained that there was no knife found, no fingerprints present, no admission by Foley, and the DNA was simply speculation. Therefore, the entire case should simply be dismissed. Look, Trooper Kevin Foley is an innocent man! Why have you arrested him? There is someone else out there who did the murder, not my client. That was Attorney Galloway's defense. He did most of the talking while Attorney Johnson watched.

On the other hand, Attorney Krastek insisted the DNA found under Dr. Yelenic's fingernails established that Kevin Foley was at 233 S. Spring Street. Entangled in close contact, Dr. Yelenic was able to reach up and scratch Foley above his left eye. There were also the admissions by his co-workers of Foley's alarming behavior following just the slightest mention of Yelenic's name for years around the Indiana Barracks.

After a vigilant eight hours, Judge Haberl ruled that there was enough evidence for the State of Pennsylvania to hold Trooper Kevin Foley for the homicide of Dr. John Yelenic. The date for Commonwealth vs Kevin James Foley in the Court of Common Pleas Indiana County of Pennsylvania #1170 Crim. 2007 was scheduled for July 15, 2008. Bail was NOT offered due to the classification of homicide. Therefore, Foley remained in the Indiana jail (across the street from the County Courthouse) until his trial date. This was a few blocks away from where Michele and the children resided.

July couldn't come soon enough. Another seven months to get through felt like another eternity. By the beginning of February 2008 Foley wanted out of jail, and the bail issue came up. It was my understanding back in November at his preliminary hearing that there was to be no bail. Now, however, his attorney was requesting a bail hearing. His mother Gail, brother James, and his aunt showed up in court only to hear Judge Martin (who was now assigned to rule on Foley's case) deny bail! That's right keep him in jail. After all, he was arrested for murder in cold blood.

To everyone's surprise, Foley's overall appearance looked as if he had been on vacation at some spa. He was sporting a tan, had gained a little weight (probably due to the jail food diet), and was dressed in a sharp well-pressed brown suit and tie, possibly compliments of his attorney. Not bad for being incarcerated for five months. His bubble had to have burst when he was once again escorted out of the courtroom in handcuffs with two guards at his sides.

Michele Yelenic was sighted visiting him from time to time, bringing *their adopted son* Gannon to see his daddy. Where was JJ in all this commotion, I wondered? He had to be confused. One dad dead and one in prison. What a mess for a nine-year-old boy to cope with. Again the cycle of a lost boy is already in motion. Where it stops . . . nobody knows.

The remaining months flew by. There were always rumors abounding. As I documented everything, whenever Mary Ann heard something, she would report it to me. During some periods, we exchanged information as frequently as two or three times daily. The burning question on everyone's mind was whether or not Michele would be arrested. Agent Regis Kelly always maintained that the case was "ongoing," giving family and friends a glimmer of hope that she, too, would be sitting in jail. Needless to say that day hasn't as yet arrived.

What did come forth during the spring of 2008 was that Attorney Galloway requested a continuance, admitting he needed more time to gather investigative evidence beneficial to the defense. Judge Martin rescheduled Foley's hearing to November 9, 2008. Upon hearing of the delay Mary Ann, Tim, Dennis, and Mag were outraged. Attorney Krastek assured everyone that Dr. Yelenic was going to get his due justice, no matter how many delays were mustered up. As a writer I thought to myself that the media must be having a field day, with all the starts and stops in this high-profile case. Next Attorney Galloway felt he wasn't going to be able to form an impartial jury in Indiana County. All these happenings had to be defense strategies taught in Continuation 101 along with Motions 101 classes because the delays did stop the case from going to trial.

At the end of October, Attorney Galloway called for another meeting in Judge Martin's chambers. This time he had changed practices and, therefore, had to bring his new partner (Jeff Monzo, who happens to be Galloway's son-in-law) up to speed in the case, as he would be second chair to him. I'll never forget Mary Ann standing in the hall shaking her head, insisting that John's case wasn't ever going to be heard. It's Indiana County! Something is up. This time even Attorney Krastek was beginning to become a believer. What a ploy. The fact of the matter was that Attorney General Tom Corbett was up for re-election in November 2008. If he should lose, then Attorney Krastek would also be relieved of his position as Deputy State Attorney General. Hence, another deputy attorney would expropriate his duties (in particular, the Yelenic case).

Everyone was holding their breath. It was clearly in the hands of voters across the state. Sure enough . . . they got a break. Attorney General Tom Corbett was re-elected. Another trial date was entered on the books at the Indiana County Courthouse for Monday, 8:30 a.m. on March 9, 2009. This time the clock was ticking loud and clear. It was affirmed . . . no turning back.

CHAPTER TWELVE

If you do the crime . . . you must do the time.

Arrivals on the first day of the trial:

March 9, 2009 began under a bleak sky and cold breezy morning as I drove from my home in Ligonier to Mary Ann's home in Blairsville. I parked my car in her driveway and jumped into the passenger seat of her car as we headed for Route 22/30, the usual routine when it came to driving to Indiana to do an interview or to go to the courthouse. A freak winter whiteout occurred about ten minutes into our trip, but nothing could stop us today from reaching that courthouse. We arrived by 8:00 a.m. giving us ample time to find a parking space and make our way to the courthouse on Philadelphia Street.

While walking up the first set of steps toward the main entrance of the courthouse, one can't help but notice a life-sized bronze statue of Indiana's native son, Jimmy Stewart, appearing to be greeting those who pass by him. Every Christmas season his Oscar award-winning film, *It's a Wonderful Life*, is viewed by generations who never seem to get tired of seeing it. It struck me that we were about to enter a courtroom stage and would see and hear how a man didn't get that second chance to live a wonderful life.

Dennis and Lisa Vaughn:

Nothing was going to keep Lisa and myself from attending Foley's trial. Once the date was set, we booked a hotel room in Indiana and made arrangements to take leaves from our jobs. We were there most of the days and fortunately, had friends like Tim and Maggie there for support. It was an excruciating experience on many levels. It was the first exposure I had had to the crime scene photos and they were devastating. I had always tried to not think about John's final minutes of life, but the pictures told a clear story that they were horrible beyond comprehension. Also, this was the first time I had ever been in the same room with Kevin Foley. I could not help but stare at his back at the defense table, wanting to either jump over the railing and strangle him or, at the very least, demand that he tell me what could possibly possess him to murder my best friend.

*****

The actual trial transcript is on file at the Indiana County courthouse

Commonweath vs Kevin James Foley
In The Court of Common Pleas Indiana County PA #1170
Crim. 2007
March 9, 2009 to March 18, 2009
The jury consisted of seven men and five women.

The following is an overview, which I have summarized, of the fifty-six witnesses testifying during the trial.

OPENING ARGUMENTS

Prosecutor:
Attorney Krastek based his approach on five points in explaining his story as to why Kevin J. Foley is accountable for the death of Dr. John Yelenic. First: the DNA under Dr. Yelenic's fingernails matched Kevin Foley; Second: Foley's outbursts of anger towards the victim and Foley's fellow troopers at the Indiana State barracks; Third: the video film footage placed Foley's SUV passing not one, but two Sheetz stores located along the drive from the Delmont ice hockey rink (where he had attended a practice) the night of April 12, 2006 into the morning of the 13th of April through Blairsville en route to Susan Drive in Indiana; Fourth: the knife that was the weapon of choice used by the assailant; Fifth: the bloody shoeprint made by an Asics Gel Creed shoe worn by Foley for years. He ended with stating to the jury that the defendant, Trooper Kevin Foley, had the motive, opportunity, and the ability to do the crime.

Defense:
Atty. Jeff Monzo began by coining the phrase "jumping to conclusion by the prosecution." Our client Kevin Foley is innocent. Why? Because there was no trace of John Yelenic's blood found in Kevin Foley's SUV. The Sheetz' video used to verify his SUV captured racing through the streets of Blairsville was inconclusive due to the poor quality of the film. As far as the DNA found and tested... it was unreliable. Basically, Kevin Foley was targeted by his supervisor because they didn't get along. Attorney Monzo also pointed out to the jury that there were at least three other persons of interest that the prosecution should have investigated. These individuals

had financial ties to Dr. John Yelenic. Early the morning of Thursday around 2:20 a.m., a neighbor residing across the street from Yelenic's house heard a man's voice yelling out, "I will never loan any money again!" He left the jury again with three simple words—jumping to conclusion.

March 9, 2009
Monday
Witnesses:

Craig Uss: Next door neighbor discovered victim's body on April 13, 2006.
Donald Isherwood: Blairsville Police Officer received 911 at 3:25 p.m. April 13, 2006.
Paula Erns: FBI agent with Field Evidence Response team studied blood patterns at crime scene (victim's house).
Charles Gonglik: Greensburg State Police processed crime scene and collected evidence.

March 10, 2009
Tuesday
Witnesses:

Cyril Wecht: Forensic pathologist gave description of how the victim was murdered in a carving fashion by a knife. Also how fragments of glass were found embedded in the skin of Yelenic's neck when his head went through a side window panel. He also explained numerous defensive wounds found on the victim's right hand, wrist, and forearm. Stating Yelenic put up a fight to live. Once the jugular vein was cut (when pushed through the window), however, he had only six or seven minutes of life. Therefore, Dr. Wecht stated the cause of death was exsanguination, which means blood is being pumped out of the body through the knife wounds, and therefore the heart is weakened when there is no longer any blood to pump.

Charles Conrad: Indiana County Deputy Coroner who assisted Blairsville Police officer Jill Gaston to report the death of Dr. John Yelenic to (his estranged wife) Michele Yelenic the night of April 13, 2006 at her residence (10 Susan Drive, Indiana, PA.).

Jill Gaston: Blairsville police officer at home of Michele Yelenic's (night of April 13, 2006) noticed a fresh red scratch mark above the left eye of Kevin Foley in the kitchen. Gaston insisted her observation was correct under oath several times. It had to be because Trooper Worcester saw it also at the Indiana barracks the morning of April 13, 2006 when he and Kevin Foley reported to work for an eight hour shift together.

Harold German Jr.: A neighbor who resides at 274 S. Spring Street, Blairsville, PA. Heard pig sounds on or about 1:00 a.m. Thursday morning April 13, 2006.

(Victim's house 233 S. Spring Street)

James Ferguson: A neighbor who resides at 247 S. Spring Street, Blairsville, PA. Heard loud sounds around 1:12 a.m. to 1:15 a.m. the Thursday morning of April 13, 2006.

Maria Alexander: A neighbor who resides at 199 S. Spring Street, Blairsville, PA. Heard a male screaming on or about 1:30 a.m./2:00 a.m. Thursday morning April 13, 2006.

Vincent Ugoletti: A neighbor who resides at 257 S. Spring Street, Blairsville, PA. Heard two male voices talking on or about 1:15a.m./1:30a.m. Thursday morning April 13, 2006.

Robert Worcester: Indiana State Police Trooper in the Crime Unit noticed a red scratch on Trooper Kevin Foley's face when he reported for duty the morning of April 13, 2006 at 8:00 a.m. They had both played hockey at practice the evening of April 12, 2006. Attorney Krastek drilled Worcester on the excuse Foley gave his co-workers about his mark. According to Worcester he was told an excuse by another trooper in the unit. Foley told him that he received the scratch from a flying hockey puck. Worcester disagreed with the officer stating Foley wears a metal face guard when he plays in the non-checking league during practice. He went on to state that he thought it was "goofy Kevin" when they were told (by Kevin) the real cause was due to him getting his hockey stick caught in his vehicle. The stick struck his face because he pulled it too hard. Attorney Krastek demonstrated several times with a hockey stick to see if he could get the same result. The jury and observers burst out laughing as Attorney Krastek tried. It seemed impossible yet alone unbelievable if you are holding the stick at arm's length to strike the face area.

March 11, 2009
Wednesday
Witnesses:

Deana Kirkland : Indiana State Police Trooper and partner of Kevin Foley. She testified to Foley's dislike towards Dr. Yelenic. She told the jury of Foley's comments while they were transferring a prisoner one day when out of the blue Foley told her that he hoped John Yelenic would be killed in a car crash. Then in 2005 Foley asked her to investigate charges brought up by Michele Yelenic in reference to John touching their son JJ during a visitation weekend. Of course, later in court the charges were dropped when JJ informed Judge Hanna that his mother told him to say that his father had touched him.

Martin Knezovich: Indiana State Police Trooper at the hockey practice April 12, 2006. Kevin Foley had played with him that evening.

John Aloi: Indiana State Police Trooper at the hockey practice April 12, 2006. Kevin Foley had played with him that evening.

Joy Goodyear: Indiana State Police Trooper noticed forehead scratch mark above Foley's eye at work April 13, 2006.

Douglas Berezansky: Indiana State Police Trooper sold Foley the hockey bag which Foley brought on April 12, 2006 to practice.

John Dell: Greensburg State Police Trooper obtained a warrant to seize hair samples from Foley.

Randall Gardner: Greensburg State Police Supervisor of Crime Unit assigned to the homicide case of Dr. John Yelenic. He was the lead investigator from the Greensburg Barracks working closely with the Attorney General's office and their investigator Agent Regin Kelly. Cpl. Gardner was also involved with the Grand Jury report turned over to the Attorney General's office prior to the arrest of Trooper Kevin Foley on September 27, 2007.

Robert Elsavage: Greensburg State Police assigned to the crime lab. He is a fabric expert analyst who examined the cut marks found on the gray sweatshirt the victim was wearing at the time of his murder. Determining what type of instrument made the cuts.

David Franks: Indiana State Police Trooper who also saw the mark on Foley's face April 13, 2006 at work.

March 12, 2009
Thursday
Witnesses:

John Brant: Blairsville Police Officer was directed by District Attorney Bob Bell to line tape the perimeter of the house at 233 S. Spring Street, Blairsville, PA. (the home of the victim/crime scene) on April 13, 2006. A few weeks later he received from Greensburg State Police Troopers Gonglik and Kendigia of the R & I Unit, a small yellow envelope containing the fingernail clippings from the victim to store at the Blairsville Police Station. He was instructed to refrigerate them. He also maintained a log of the crime scene, recording all personnel who arrived (time) at 233 S. Spring Street.

Michael Hochrein: FBI Agent at Quantico, Va. who Cpl. R. Gardner sent victim's nail clippings down to be analyzed.

Jerrilyn Conway: FBI Agent at Quantico, Va. Analyst of DNA matching. She noted a 90 % match to Dr. Yelenic and a 10% match to Foley.

Dr. Robin Cotton: Professor at Boston University School of Medicine stated she found there was a one-in-23 million chance that the DNA sample studied from Dr. Yelenic matched someone *other than* Kevin Foley.

Dr. Mark Perlin: CEO of Cybergenetics, Pittsburgh, PA. claimed even a higher probability of 189 billion. Of course, we were reminded that the more advanced the computer software used to analyze the DNA, the higher the numbers would become.

Barbara Swasy: Her husband, Roger, is first cousin to John Yelenic. She was a friend of Michele Yelenic and invited to the wedding of John and Michele that took place in LasVegas in December of 1997. Barbara phoned Michele late afternoon of April 13, 2006 to report to her that she was informed that John Yelenic was found dead in his home. "John's gone, John's gone," were her exact words to Michele. She told Kevin to go over to the house and find out what had happened. The witness then stated that Kevin told her that Blairsville was out of his jurisdiction. Therefore, he was not permitted to interfere in the investigations.

Regin Kelly ------ -------- ----------- -----------

March 13, 2009
Friday
Witnesses:

Terry Schalow: Asics American Corporation, he is a Product Marketing manager for Performance Running Shoes. He provided information on shoe treads, in particular the Gel

Creed Plus style Trooper Kevin Foley wore. The treads of the Gel Creed Plus sole matched the shoeprints found at the crime scene throughout the first floor (kitchen, dining room, living room, hallway). He also produced the order form used by Foley with his credit card number, address (his own home at 275 Charles Street, Indiana, Pa.) and home/job phone numbers appearing.

All exhibits were displayed for the jury verification.

- Michael Smith: FBI agent assigned to the laboratory department in Quantico, VA. He is a forensic examiner who studies shoeprint and tire print impressions. He examined the shoeprints from the body to the kitchen door of 233 S. Spring Street.
- Russell States: A Loss Investigator Supervisor for Sheetz Incorporated out of the home office of Altoona. His duty is to confirm that all radio systems are working correctly as well as cameras inside and outside of stores. He stated the Blairsville Police Department requested to view videos from the New Alexandra Sheetz and the Blairsville Sheetz on April 13, 2006. All stores situated on Route 119 and north of Route 22 were of interest because they sit between Blairsville.
- Robert Harr: Greensburg State Police Trooper with the Criminal Investigation Unit worked with Cpl. Gardner and the video surveillance tapes from several Sheetz stores.

  He narrated from the film the headlights of a SUV, reddish that resembled Foley's on April 13, 2006 traveling from the Delmont Ice Rink toward Blairsville at 12:18:05 a.m. onto E. Market Street where the Blairsville Sheetz is located. The time and speed was calculated to determine the travel range.
- Randall Gardner: Called again to testify in a re-enactment of the route taken by Kevin Foley.
- Amanda Broyles: FBI in the Operational Technology division for the forensic video, audio, and image analysis unit. She compared vehicles on digital video film of Foley's SUV

passing the New Alexandra Sheetz and the Blairsville Sheetz with a known image (the photo) of his SUV. Her conclusion was due to the high compression of the film it resulted in making it extremely difficult to compare it with the Sheetz surveillance and the re-enacted one. However, she would not include or exclude the known vehicle as being the questioned vehicle in the two videos.

March 16, 2009
Monday
Witnesses:

Effie Alexander: The attorney for Dr. John Yelenic's divorce preparation since 2004. She worked out with John the details of the filing, which was to take place upon him signing the final Marital Settlement Agreement sent to him. Yelenic arranged to have it witnessed by his aunt, uncle, and cousin Mary Ann Clark at a notary's office in Blairsville on April 13, 2006 at 3:00 p.m. She informed the jury of her assistance in the alleged molestation case against John, PFA charges, and his custody struggles. She tried to explain the financial arrangements of property, business holdings from the dental practice, life insurance policy, and retirement accounts, together worth over 1.6 million dollars. Michele Yelenic was the beneficiary of the life insurance policy. As of April 13, 2006 John Yelenic had NOT changed the beneficiary. He was going to do that after the agreement (marital) had been signed and filed. However, John Yelenic's estate is maintaining all funds to be issued to the primary heir, and will be dispensed to JJ on his eighteenth birthday.

Robert Bell: District Attorney for Indiana County, PA. Indiana was first notified of the homicide by Coroner Mike Baker. Bell was contacted next by Sgt. Emigh of the Indiana State Police who asked if the State Police would need to respond to the scene. Bell had arrived at 233 S. Spring Street at the same time (4:00 p.m.) as Chief Hess had arrived. Hess advised Bell that Blairsville Police would maintain jurisdiction of the investigation and presently he did not need any assistance. Bell went on to discuss the numerous cell calls he had received from Sgt. Emigh. Informing Bell of a live-in relationship Kevin Foley had with Yelenic's soon to be ex-wife Michele for years. Bell also mentioned a dislike Sgt. Emigh had for Foley. When asked by the prosecution if he knew a knife was involved, Bell indicated not to his knowledge; he was cognizant that a window was involved. On page 58 of the transcript, Sgt. Emigh believed firmly that a search warrant should have been issued that night (April 13, 2006). Bell stated there was no probable cause for a search warrant to be issued. However, on the other hand, Bell continued to insist on Chief Hess turning the Yelenic homicide over to the Special Crime Unit of the State Police. Why? Because they had over 30 State Troopers to thoroughly investigate the case, while Blairsville borough had six officers and many were not trained for this type of case. By the summer of 2006, Hess turned over the case to the State Police due to mounting frustration from those investigating the case as well as family and friends. Since Sgt. Emigh was serving at the Indiana Barracks, the chief law enforcement officials and officer of Indiana County redirected the investigation to be turned over to the Greensburg State Police facility. Months later Sgt. Emigh's retirement took place.

Daniel Lovette: Attorney for Michele Yelenic who was involved with negotiations of the settlement issues in the divorce. At one point the property proceeds was a huge issue. Then when the sixty/forty split (Michele 60/John 40) came into play, the property issues didn't seem to be a problem. A tentative agreement had been reached very late in 2005. However, it had not been drafted nor signed. Therefore, bargaining was still in progress up until February of 2006. There were issues in the Marital Settlement Agreement that John was questioning, pertaining to how much support he would pay Michele and JJ. The new Marital Settlement Agreement went from $3,700 a month to almost half that. On page 76 of his testimony, Lovette outlines the petitions needed for Judge Hanna to hear before the Marital Settlement Agreement could be signed. Regardless, Michele *did* signed it in March 2006. Lovette had her affidavit of consent to waiver of notice. Therefore, Michele Yelenic agreed to the divorce and he had received the documents in his office early April 2006. Michele made an appointment to come to his office to sign the agreement, and Lovette in turn forwarded it to Attorney Effie Alexander. Who then contacted John Yelenic that she would be sending the final document for him to sign before a notary and return to her office to file?

Isaiah Brader: He lived across the street in an apartment building facing the Yelenic house. He heard two voices coming from across the street, one louder than the other. The louder voice stated that he would never loan money to them. He heard glass shattering. At one point he thought it was the garbage truck throwing out glass.

Melissa Uss: Next door neighbor at 227 S. Spring Street. She and her husband Tom went to high school with John Yelenic. They were very good friends whom John had advanced $15,000.00 for Melissa to open up a bakery in Blairsville. Yelenic asked for the check to be returned early in April because he needed the funds for his 2005 taxes since Michele decided to file single, claiming the children as *her* dependents. That caused John's taxes due to become increasingly higher. Since much of his assets were being liquidated due to the settlement with Michele, he needed that loan back. Much of the testimony under cross-examination was based on the check and her husband's shoe size and where he buys his shoes.

Pamela Ferguson: Neighbor at 235 S. Spring Street, Blairsville saw Melissa and Yelenic sitting on his porch talking or standing on sidewalk talking. The morning hours of April 13, 2006 she was awakened by hearing yelling around

12:30 a.m. The issue of grass cutting of Yelenic's yard was focused on. Tom Uss began cutting the grass after April 14, 2006. The clippings were collected in a blue barrel and Melissa Uss' father's truck was used to haul them away. Then she told about one day observing Melissa opening the trunk of her car and taking out a tote bag then handing it to another lady who had parked her car behind Melissa. Then they drove away.

Darla Ferguson: Much conversation was done at sidebar. Attorney Galloway had subpoenaed this witness. He asked her if she had stated prior if Melissa Uss and Dr. Yelenic's interactions occurred while Tom Uss was not living at the house. Darla responded by saying that Tom was away in the Navy. She went on to say that Melissa was lonely/going through hard times while Yelenic was in the process of a divorce. They both were supporting each other. Attorney Galloway slipped in a statement asking Darla if it was fair to say she never saw them holding hands, kissing or showing any intimate moves. She answered . . . no, no she had not. There was a further sidebar that Attorney Galloway requested after the witness was dismissed.

David Okopal: Indiana State Police Trooper who commented on the relationship of Sgt. Emigh and Trooper Kevin Foley as being tumultuous and rocky. He was asked if Kevin Foley bought sneakers for others in his barracks. He was then asked what size shoe he wears. Okopal responded, that he wore a ten and a half. Then he was asked if Kevin's shoe size was larger or smaller. Larger to his knowledge. However, he didn't know Kevin's boot size.

John Ogden: A retired police officer from El Segundo, California. Returned to Indiana where he was the Chief of Police for Indiana Borough. He had known Kevin Foley for five years. Met him through the youth hockey program in Indiana that his two sons and Michele's son Nathan played in. Attorney Galloway asked if Foley's reputation would be one of being a good, peaceful, law-abiding citizen? Ogden answered in his opinion Foley has always been looked at as a very good citizen, peaceful. He is always cool and very calm.

Janet Ogden: A retired police officer from Hawthorne, California. Now employed as an administrative assistant with the S&T Bank in downtown Indiana. She agreed with Kevin being a law abiding, peaceful, gentle person that people entrusted their children to, such as the Allegheny Badgers Organization (hockey team).

March 17, 2009
Tuesday
Witnesses:

Dr. Laurence Mueller: Genetics professor at the University of California at Irvine. Discussed thresholds that labs will not go because of scientific reliability concerns while interpreting the alleles count consistent in an individual's DNA. Called by the defense, Mueller responded to findings of the FBI, Dr. Cotton, and Dr. Perlin. In Mueller's findings he focused on the mixture making up DNA in the overall population. Much of the research was done by students, not himself.

Jack Edmundson: Indiana County Corner did the removal of the body of Dr. Yelenic from the home. He commented on the public interest that had gathered on the sidewalk and street area.

Timothy Lipniskis: Indiana State Police Trooper who did the coach-pupil segment of the training of Kevin Foley on or about 1994. The process lasted 150 days. Foley was assigned to the crime unit, but he couldn't verify the date. When asked about Foley's reputation, he also agreed with the defense. Kevin Foley is a good law abiding citizen, truthful, and honest.

Christopher Adams: Indiana State Police Trooper again agreed with the defense when asked about Kevin Foley's reputation.

Russell States: Again questioned by the defense on why the camera could not pick out the SUV en route through Homer City or Black Lick. According to States, if the camera system is in the proper position, it will pick out vehicles passing by. Much of the concerns were the cameras in Blairsville and New Alexander, questioning if they are were on different systems.

Rev. Standford Webb: He was a friend of Kevin Foley. When asked by defense if Foley's reputation was that of being truthful and honest, Webb commented that he knew Foley personally. Just personally.

Recess at 11:22 a.m.: In the Chambers with Judge Martin , Attorneys Krastek and Galloway discussed the past, present, and future case status. Referring to pages 83 through 100.

Marsha Delaney: A real estate agent in Indiana. Met Foley in March 2005. Again agreed with the defense of Foley's reputation as being good in the community.

Michael Supinka: An attorney in Indiana knew Foley through their managing a little league team together as well as hockey games. His son played with Michele Yelenic's son, Nathan. He also agreed with Foley's reputation as being good. The same for truthful and a honest person.

William Bagley: A prisoner in the Westmoreland County Jail who stated that he heard another prisoner claim responsibility for the doctor's death.

Michael McElfresh: Greensburg State Police Trooper for the Crime Investigation Unit who interviewed Bagley as well as Brian Ray, the prisoner who claimed he was responsible for Yelenic's death.

A sidebar: On page 121 through 142 discussing Brian Ray, polygraph, DNA, witness Darla Ferguson, Melissa Uss, Galloway's theory that Tom Uss is the one who murdered Dr. Yelenic (page 138). The complete Attorney Galloway theory is presented in the presence of Judge Martin and Attorney Krastek throughout 21 pages.

Jacquelin McCraken: An attorney and one-time Assistant District Attorney for Indiana County. Agreed that Foley had a very good reputation, as being truthful and a trustworthy person. As a trooper he dedicated his life to upholding the law.

Sarah King: Resides at 12 Susan Drive. A neighbor of Michele Yelenic and Kevin Foley of 10 Susan Drive. She concluded that she had not heard anything negative about Foley in the neighborhood.

March 18, 2009
Wednesday
Witnesses:

Kevin Foley: Is sworn in and takes the stand.

Under direct examination by Attorney Galloway on page 4:
Overview of his early life growing up in Schroon Lake, N.Y., then moving to Fort Richey, Florida. Life with Michele Maygar-Kamler-Yelenic. His Gel Creed running shoe. Hockey practice the night of April 12 into April 13, 2006. How he felt about George Emigh, his supervisor at the Indiana Barracks. Adopting his son Gannon from Guatemala. The warrant to search 10 Susan Drive, taking his DNA, and computer. The clothes he wore the evening of April 12, 2006. His knife collection and usage.

Under cross examination by Attorney Krastek on page 95:
How Foley met Michele Magyar-Kamler-Yelenic. Asking Trooper Deana Kirkland to investigate the molestation claim Michele filed against John Yelenic. Also Foley asking Kirkland to pray Yelenic dies in a car crash. Telling Trooper Daniel Zenisek that he wished Yelenic to get killed. Discussed Foley's 10 1/2 shoe size and his ordering of Gel Creed on his credit card. The number of knives he owned and where he stored them. His habit of

playing with his knife at work (flicking it open and closed and at other troopers). Foley's route back to Indiana the night of April 12 into April 13, 2006 from the hockey arena in Delmont. No problems with John Yelenic when exchanging JJ during visitations since May 2005. Conversation with Barb Swasy at a fish fry April 7, 2006 based on custody issues between Michele and John. According to Michele everything had been taken care of during a meeting at Valley Dairy in Blairsville among Michele, Attorney Lovette (her attorney), John, and Attorney Alexander weeks ago. Back to Foley wishing for Yelenic's demise with Trooper Kirkland. The evening of April 13, 2006 when Officer Jill Gaston went to 10 Susan Drive to tell Michele Yelenic of the death of her husband, John Yelenic. Also asking about the fresh scratch she noticed above his eye. Attorney Krastek's demonstration of how the hockey stick blade could have scratched Foley while he was trying to place it into the SUV (under Foley's direction). It appeared to be impossible to do as Attorney Krastek tried several different ways.

Redirect by Attorney Galloway:

Back to what JJ told Michele which caused Michele to file the molestation claim against John. Asking Foley why Sgt. Emigh was suspended from the State Police. Just joking around with Trooper Zenisek about wishing Yelenic would die. Just joking. Accompanying Trooper Erdely to Michele's home to investigate the e-mail hacking charges brought against her by a male friend of hers. Foley's threats against Yelenic (he claimed) he had no intentions to carry out. No blood was found on the shoes taken from his home. No fingerprints were found of Foley's at the scene of the crime. Foley stated he did not hate Dr. John Yelenic nor did he show any violence (carry out) toward Yelenic.

Recross by Atty. Krastek:

Questioning Foley's recall of what he said to Trooper Zenisek, Tropper Kirkland, and Barb Swasy. Note on page

150 about all the jokes Foley states in the past. Now Dr. John Yelenic winds up dead!

Redirect by Atty. Galloway:
Asked Foley how many DNA requests did he investigate in his law enforcement career. No outside consultants were ever used because the samples were sent to the PSP/DNA lab to seek matches.

A sidebar was called: Between Attorneys Galloway, Krastek, and Judge Martin.

Kevin Foley stepped down ending his testimony.

At 1:15 p.m. both defense and prosecution at rest with no rebuttals when asked by Judge Martin. Therefore, Judge Martin proceeds to inform the jury that closing arguments will follow. They began with Attorney Monzo then Attorney Krastek, which can be found on pages 162 through 240 of the record of proceedings #1170 Crim. 2007 Commonweath vs Kevin James Foley

3:38 p.m.: Jury dismissed to deliberate. The courtroom was then cleared.

8:08 p.m.: Request for definition of reasonable doubt.

10:10 p.m.: Verdict reached by jury

VERDICT: On the charge of murder in the first degree, we find the defendant . . . GUILTY!

Atty. Galloway: Requested a poll. After the poll by the court the verdict was affirmed.

Judge Martin: Dismissed the jurors at 10:06 p.m. He then instructed sentencing in the matter for June 1, 2009 at 8:30 a.m. in his courtroom.

Court was now adjourned.

As an author, this was definitely a moment I will always cherish. After two years of investigating and documenting the highs and lows—of the family, friends, and law enforcement—watching the reaction was mystical. As if everyone in the room had guilty on their minds (except a few) then the actual word was spoken by the jury foreman. Tears ran down the faces of family members, friends, and even some of the media reporters who had been with the Dr. John Yelenic case since April 13, 2006. Foley just sat in his chair motionless. Chief Hess let out a loud YES and jumped to his feet while others embraced. I was seated by Melissa and Tom Uss whom the defense had kept hammering away at over the years. Tom's reaction was one of bewilderment, while Melissa wiped tears from her eyes. Finally it was all over. Trooper Kevin Foley had finally met up with his fate.

We all exited the courtroom, some taking the stairs while others waited for the elevators. The crowd went out the front doors of the courthouse to be greeted by television cameras and newspaper reporters just waiting to capture our reactions live.

Mary Ann Clark cried as she expressed her sincere thanks to the justice system and all those who stood tall, fighting to convict the murderer of her cousin Dr. John Yelenic on April 12, 2006, the night before he was to sign his divorce papers to end a very bitter marriage.

Dennis Vaughn's reaction to the verdict:

Never taking away for a moment my conviction that Foley was guilty from the moment I heard of the murder, the evidence presented so masterfully at the trial by Anthony Krastek was rock solid in my opinion. Could the jury not see that? Hour after hour passed with no word from the jury, other than them requesting a definition of the phrase "reasonable doubt." None of us thought that was a positive sign.

The sun had long set and we were just starting to think that the jury deliberations were going to carry over to the next day when we received word that the verdict had come in. We raced back to our seats in the courtroom and watched for any sign of how they might have voted as the jurors were led back into the room. After what seemed like an eternity of procedural language, the verdict was finally read. "Guilty of First Degree Murder" may have been the sweetest words I had ever heard. Finally, someone was going to be held responsible for John's murder.

CHAPTER THIRTEEN

To avoid loss don't attach anything to it.

On the morning of June 1, 2009, I thought I was dreaming. But here we were to witness the final moment of justice, the *sentencing phase*. As I glanced around the silent courtroom . . . where were Kevin Foley's supporters? His attorneys were seated beside him as they were back in March. Where were Michele, Nicole, Nathan, James Foley (his brother), Karen Peck (his twin sister), and Foley's dedicated colleagues? They were nowhere in sight as he sat dressed up in a suit between his defense team. I wonder what was going through his mind.

As a member of the audience, I recalled staring above Judge Martin's bench during the trial to a message displayed on the wall that read, "No man is above the law and no man is below it." Now it was Foley's turn to face the reality of the justice system, which would begin as the gavel came down. Not just yet for there is one more step to complete this chapter—the reading of letters to the judge written by those who knew the victim. These letters are called "impact statements." The point is to show how their lives had been altered by the hand of the defendant. I have included several of the ones read to the court as well as others.

Fighting back tears, several friends and family members read their letters out loud. One by one each expressed the trauma Dr. John Yelenic had to deal with on a daily basis throughout the years. A total of six letters were selected. Why those particular ones? I have my thoughts, but you can read a sample of them for yourself. Dr. Maria Tacelosky (who went to dental school with JohnYelenic) was the first to stand before Judge Martin and read, followed by Susan Coates (neighbor on S. Spring Street/friend), Roberta (Bobbi) Mack, Dennis Vaughn (college friend), Maggie McCartin (friend), and Mary Ann Clark (cousin).

Attorney Galloway jumped up out of his seat twice during Mary Ann's reading of her letter to object. Why? Perhaps she revealed John Yelenic as a real person. There was no jury present to hear any particular details which had been completely held back from the jury throughout the trial. That issue haunted me as a documentarian. There was *never* a human side of John Yelenic for the public to hear or a picture of him with his son JJ during happier times, which is one reason why I wanted to write his story. Even John Magyar (brother of Michele) expressed his compassion for John in his impact letter. Too bad his wasn't selected to be read out loud on the day of Kevin Foley's sentencing. It is also excluded from this book, per John Magyar's request of January 25, 2013 when I interviewed him by phone. His letter, however, is on file at the Indiana courthouse with the other impact letters submitted.

At the end, Judge Martin spoke to the court. He expressed logic that I'm sure so many wished Kevin Foley had used that fatal evening of April 12, 2006. It left many to ponder the what ifs: "You could have reconsidered your decisions at any point while driving to Blairsville from Delmont. When turning on to S. Spring Street the street Dr. John Yelenic lived on. While placing your car in park then turning the engine off. Getting out of the car then walking toward the steps leading up to the kitchen door of his home. Reaching for the door knob, turning it, then entering. You had time to *reflect* and *stop*."

The oath taken to become a Pennsylvania State Police officer was breached. Incomprehensible is the word Judge Martin used to describe Kevin Foley's actions as a fifteen-year veteran officer of law enforcement. Reprehensible action taken by one human being to another. Greed described the root of this heinous crime done to Dr. Yelenic. Then in an instant the sentence followed. Life imprisonment . . . no probation . . . echoed out! Followed by a loud response from Chief Hess seated in the center row of the courtroom. Now Kevin Foley would live the remainder of his life tucked away within the walls of a 9' by 11' cell in the solitary confinement section of a state correction facility. The victim is in a coffin at the Blairsville cemetery. Where is the third person, Michele Yelenic, in this story?

After the sentencing, I suggested a drive up to Michele's house on Susan Drive to see if her car was parked in the driveway. So off we went with Mary Ann driving Dr. Maria, Gus, and myself. To our amazement a pickup truck was parked in the driveway loaded up with furniture. Nathan and a few of his buddies could be seen carrying items from a side door of the house to the truck.

Michele's voice could be heard coming out from the inside of the garage.

    I took my video camera out of its case, leaping out of the car to the street to film their departure while it was in progress. Standing in the driveway of house next door I began filming. It was a nice well-kept home in an upscale neighborhood in Indiana, PA back in 2007 when I first filmed it. Now in 2009, it appeared be in dire need of a paint job as well as repairs to the windows, doors, and deck in the back. That once manicured lawn, shrubs, and flowers had perished throughout the years. Since Foley's imprisonment back in the fall of 2007, care of the house, money, and protection had come to a halt. Discarded and now abandoned is how the game is played. John Yelenic was discarded while Kevin Foley is now abandoned. JJ is still in the game so far.

    The moral of Dr. John Yelenic's story is once you accept evil into your life, it will consume your soul until it perishes. If you're lucky . . . you may get away with your LIFE. Take this lesson from one . . . that didn't!

Dennis Vaughn's final thoughts:

    Foley's sentencing a few months later was anticlimactic in the sense that we were already informed that the death penalty was off the table in this case, and that the only remaining option was life in prison with no chance of parole. I thought that was just fine. A life in prison for a former state trooper would be an ordeal. Maybe Foley would finally get a taste of the fear and intimidation that John had suffered at his hands. The most noteworthy part of the sentencing hearing was that it gave many of us an opportunity to speak in court regarding how John's murder affected us. For the first time, John's friends and family could finally speak out about what all this meant to us and, speaking at least for myself, it did bring about a small amount of catharsis. Foley, who had never met me before, got to hear from me just what I thought about his crime and the cost that I have been forced to pay in losing my best friend. I sincerely hope these words, as well as the words of others who spoke that day, echo in his mind for the rest of his life. He will have plenty of time to reflect on them.

    Life goes on for those of us who survived this ordeal, and I have learned many valuable life lessons as a result. I will never take for granted the loved ones I am fortunate to have in my life. I know now that they could be taken away literally overnight. I have also learned that justice can be a relative term. I have wrestled with myself in trying to decide if I feel that justice has been served in this case. On one hand, Foley is paying a very hefty price for what he did. It won't bring John back, but some satisfaction can be derived from knowing that Foley is forced to sacrifice his freedom every day for John's murder. On the other hand, I am still plagued by my suspicions that others may have culpability in John's death and these people may never be brought to justice. I find it hard to believe that Kevin Foley's drive to murder John was derived solely from his own thoughts and opinions. I suspect that his mind and heart may have been poisoned along the way, driving him to commit an act that he thought, in his twisted and distorted view, was righteous. If it can be shown that his thoughts were corrupted by falsehoods, exaggerations, and outright lies, does it not follow that the source of this corruption also shares some of the responsibility for John's death? I cannot rest until there is resolution of this question.

Without resolution, justice cannot be served, in my opinion.

CHAPTER FOURTEEN

The Blairsville Slaying and the Dawn of DNA Computing

Mark W. Perlin, PhD, MD, PhD
Cybergenetics, Pittsburgh, PA 15213

Murder

On April 13, 2006, Blairsville dentist Dr. John Yelenic was murdered in his home, about an hour east of Pittsburgh, PA. Dr. Yelenic, who was living alone at the time, had exsanguinated onto his living room floor. On the coffee table, splattered with his blood, was the unsigned divorce document from his estranged wife, Michele. She was living with her boyfriend, Pennsylvania State Trooper Kevin Foley.

John Yelenic's fingernails had DNA that tied Trooper Foley to the crime, with a match statistic of 13,000. Prior to Mr. Foley's February 2008 preliminary hearing, his defense lawyer Richard Galloway said that the DNA did not rule out other suspects, because there was a one in 13,000 chance it came from someone else. Moreover, said his lawyer, DNA often identifies suspects to the exclusion of billions or trillions of others.

Computer

I was intrigued by Mr. Galloway's dismissal of the DNA match statistic. In my research as a scientist at Cybergenetics, a small Pittsburgh DNA technology firm, we had seen that computer interpretation of DNA mixtures usually preserves more identification information than does human review. Validation studies had compared our TrueAllele® computer interpretation method with human expert review of the same DNA data, and typically showed a million-fold improvement in the match statistic. In the Foley case, that factor of a million could correct a 13,000 statistic into the billions, a level that the defense would find compelling.

Cybergenetics contacted the Pennsylvania prosecutor, Senior Deputy Attorney General Anthony Krastek, whose office is in Pittsburgh, and told him about our TrueAllele technology. When I spoke with SDAG Krastek, I explained to him how the computer could examine the DNA evidence far more carefully than could any person, and how that enhanced data scrutiny would objectively produce a more accurate match statistic. In our experience, when a person reported a DNA match in the thousands, the computer often found a statistic in the billions. SDAG Krastek arranged to send us the electronic data evidence that had been produced by the FBI laboratory in Quantico, Virginia.

I met with SDAG Krastek in Cybergenetics' Oakland office on Friday, April 11, 2008. He handed me a compact disc (CD) containing the FBI's DNA data. We discussed the case and the TrueAllele computer approach. The forensic problem was that there was a vast amount of the victim's DNA, combined with a small quantity of a second, unknown contributor.

Cybergenetics put the electronic DNA mixture data into its TrueAllele machine, asking the computer to solve the problem, and help identify the unknown contributor. The computer worked on our questions over the weekend. On Monday morning, I reviewed the results and phoned SDAG Krastek with the TrueAllele answer. The DNA under Dr. Yelenic's fingernails matched Kevin Foley with a statistic in the hundreds of billions. Further calculations would later refine this number to 189 billion.

DNA

Deoxyribonucleic acid (DNA) is the genetic blueprint passed down from parent to child that encodes the human operating system. Whereas computers represent instructions in a binary format of zeros and ones, DNA uses a four letter nucleotide alphabet of A, C, G and T. Three billion DNA letters instruct our cells on how to live, grow, reproduce and die.

A person's DNA is packaged into 23 chromosome pairs, with one copy inherited from each parent (Figure 1). The DNA sentence at a chromosome location (or, "locus"), is called an "allele". Except for the female (X) and male (Y) chromosomes, a person has two alleles (one from each parent) at every genetic locus. A person's allele pair at a locus is called a "genotype".

Figure 1

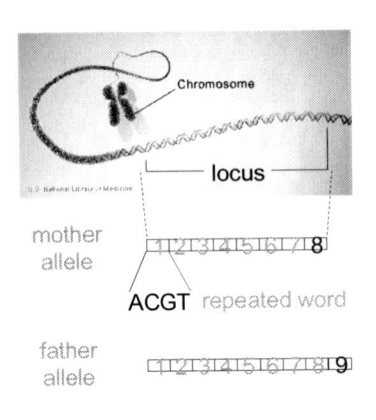

Human chromosomes come in pairs. The diagram shows a chromosome at different levels of magnification. The full chromosome has been unraveled to drill down to the individual DNA letters. A genetic locus used for forensic identification is made of Short (e.g., four letter) DNA words that are Tandemly Repeated (STR) to form a DNA sentence. The length of a person's DNA sentence at an STR locus is called an "allele". Two alleles (e.g., an "8" from one parent, and a "9" from the other parent) form this person's (8,9) allele pair "genotype".

Whereas functional genes are DNA sentences that code for proteins in the cellular machinery, other tracts of DNA have no known purpose. This "junk" DNA has highly variable regions with many different allele possibilities at a locus. Forensic scientists use junk DNA "loci" (plural form of locus) to identify people, since these loci have very many different allele pair possibilities—the chance that two people share the same two alleles is low.

Mixtures

A person's genotype is comprised of two alleles at a genetic locus. This allele pair shows up in the DNA data as one or two peaks (the two alleles could be the same). Peak size (x-axis) indicates the allele, while peak height (y-axis) is related to the quantity of allele present. A DNA mixture combines allele pairs from each contributor to the evidence. Nature adds up these allele pair DNA molecules in proportion to their contribution to produce a data pattern (Figure 2).

Figure 2

The crime laboratory transforms biological evidence into DNA data, the black curve shown in the figure. A DNA peak has a size (measured on the x-axis) that indicates the number of repeated words, and thus the allele value. The peak also has a height (measured on the y-axis) that reflects the amount of that allele present in the DNA evidence. This DNA mixture data is from the D7S820 (aka, "D7") locus in the Foley case fingernail evidence. The two tall peaks (8,12) correspond to the 93% major genotype contribution of victim John Yelenic. The two small peaks (10,13) correspond to a 7% minor genotype contribution from someone else. Kevin Foley's D7 genotype is (10,13), and so matches the minor evidence genotype. The *inclusion* interpretation of this data did not use Dr. Yelenic's (8,12) genotype, and so yielded relatively little match information; the *subtraction* and *addition* methods did use the victim's genotype, and were thus far more informative.

Computer interpretation of a DNA mixture is easy to understand. The computer tries out virtually every possible allele pair for the DNA contributors, adding them up in various proportions. Those genotypes (and their amounts) that better explain the data have a greater likelihood of being true. Sophisticated methods like TrueAllele consider many other variables, and also determine the uncertainty of every variable. After many thousands of computer proposals and comparisons, a genotype is developed for every contributor at each tested genetic locus. This evidence genotype provides the probability of each allele pair. The computer-inferred genotype is completely objective, because no knowledge of any suspect is used in its determination.

In contrast, human experts tackle DNA mixture problems in a far simpler way. People cannot cope with the full complexity of all conceivable allele pairs, and the many possible combinations and sums. Nor can they explore all the feasible allele peak patterns. The analysts do not use the original peak height data, but instead declare that each allele is either present or absent. This imperfect decision is based on whether a data peak lies above or below some "threshold" value.

The examiner then asks whether a suspect's allele pair is included in the list of alleles that appear to be present in the data. This "inclusion" method discards considerable information, and can give wrong answers, but it is the most popular approach used by human experts when they examine DNA mixtures. With John Yelenic's fingernails, inclusion gave a match statistic of 13,000 to Kevin Foley.

TrueAllele's "addition" method uses peak height data, along with the fact that the victim's DNA can be present in his own fingernails. The threshold-based "inclusion" method does not use this available data.

There is a middle ground—subtracting out the victim's genotype, though still not using peak heights. For a third opinion, Prosecutor Krastek brought in Dr. Robin Cotton, former scientific director of the Cellmark forensic DNA laboratory. Her "subtraction" interpretation of the Yelenic fingernail mixture evidence produced a DNA match of 23 million to Trooper Foley.

Law

The scientific basis of informative DNA match statistics is the likelihood ratio (LR). The LR is a number that tells us how much more probable a match between evidence and a person is than mere coincidence. The mathematics of the LR helps ensure that this match number removes preconceptions and prejudices unrelated to the evidence.

Forensic DNA scientists test many (e.g., 10 to 15) independent genetic loci for more identification power. They multiply together the match statistics from these independent genetic loci to form a product, often quite a large number. This multiplication is called the "product rule".

In Pennsylvania, the product rule became a precedent for DNA evidence in the Commonwealth vs. Blasioli rape case. In 1996, the Superior Court held in its Blasioli decision that the product rule was generally accepted within the scientific community, and that statistical evidence derived from that method was admissible. The Pennsylvania Supreme Court affirmed that determination in 1998. Thus, new human or computer methods for calculating product rule LRs for DNA match may arise, but the foundational product rule itself is not novel under Pennsylvania case law.

Challenge

Foley's defense team challenged the TrueAllele computer interpretation. They claimed that the approach (which employs the product rule) was novel science, and thus Judge Martin should first determine its reliability before the findings could be admitted as evidence. The prosecution disagreed, maintaining that the product rule was not novel in Pennsylvania. Regardless, a pretrial hearing was held to determine (a) whether an admissibility hearing was actually needed, and (b) if it was necessary, whether TrueAllele was sufficiently reliable to allow the 189 billion DNA match statistic to be heard by the jury. Since TrueAllele had never been used or challenged in court, I began preparing a presentation that would explain to the judge why TrueAllele was scientifically reliable.

The February 18, 2009 pretrial hearing was held on a wintry Wednesday before presiding Judge William Martin. The Indiana County Courthouse is on Philadelphia Street, adjacent to the Jimmy Stewart Museum. Judge Martin was the evidentiary gatekeeper responsible for determining whether or not TrueAllele would be admitted as scientific evidence in his trial. Sitting without a jury, the judge would hear testimony and review exhibits, presented through direct and cross-examination, and then render his admissibility decision.

Reliability

Prosecutor Krastek began by asking me about the principles of DNA mixture interpretation. I explained that, fundamentally, all interpretation methods, whether done by man or machine, operated in the same way. First, a genotype is inferred from the DNA data, by comparing hypothesized models with the data in order to determine the probabilities of each genotype explanation. Then, this evidence genotype (as a probability distribution) is compared to a reference genotype (e.g., Kevin Foley), relative to a population, to calculate a DNA match statistic called a "likelihood ratio".

- Mixture interpretation methods are all the same in principle, but differ in how much use they make of the available data.
- The FBI's *inclusion* method does not use the victim's DNA genotype. Moreover, inclusion does not use the original quantitative data, it reduces data peaks to all-or-none "allele" events.
- Dr. Cotton's *subtraction* method does use the victim genotype. However, like inclusion, her method does not use the peak heights.
- The TrueAllele computer's *addition* method makes the most use of the evidence, and considers both the victim genotype, as well as the quantitative height of the data peaks.
- Using more data can preserve more identification information.

Pennsylvania applies the "Frye standard" for determining the admissibility of scientific evidence. Based on a 1923 court decision, Frye v. United States, judges use this reliability standard to assess the general acceptance of a method in a relevant scientific community.

I showed that TrueAllele is based on established science, as published in scientific journals. SDAG Krastek provided the court with a CD containing almost 50 such articles. I reviewed with the judge a bibliography that listed these articles, describing TrueAllele's scientific foundations. The topics included DNA peak heights, genotype probability, DNA computer interpretation, statistical modeling and computing, likelihood ratios, similar computer systems, and my own publications.

A validation study is done to establish the scientific reliability of a method. I showed Judge Martin a TrueAllele validation study from a 2006 conference paper of mine.

This study compared different mixture interpretation methods, and found TrueAllele to be more informative (as measured by higher DNA match statistics) than human review of the same data. We went over newer validation results (that were published later in 2009) done on 40 DNA mixtures of known composition. These results (from data unrelated to the case) could be used to predict the match statistic in the Foley case, based on the amount of DNA in the 7% minor contributor to the fingernail evidence. The results predicted that the computer's match statistic would be around a trillion, while human methods would be far less informative.

The reason why people lose information is the all-or-none "threshold" that human analysts apply to DNA data in order to simplify mixture interpretation. To explain the impact of thresholds, I showed a pure black and white (high contrast) photograph of a face; we could see that the person was a young man—and little else. I then showed the judge the original image with all its shades of gray restored, revealing the face of a young Jimmy Stewart, as he looked in his classic film *It's a Wonderful Life*. It was visually apparent that using more of the data can retain far more information.

Indeed, that is how the forensic DNA scientific community contrasts simple inclusion with more powerful likelihood ratio methods. I showed the judge a highly influential 2006 paper written by the DNA Commission of the International Society for Forensic Genetics (ISFG). The article quotes prominent scientists as saying that the inclusion method:

> - "Often robs the items of any probative value" (Dr. Bruce Weir)

- "Usually discards a lot of information compared to the correct likelihood ratio approach" (Dr. Charles Brenner)
- "Does not use as much of the information included in the data as the LR approach but, conceptually, they are equivalent" (Dr. Michael Krawczak)

The ISFG Commission's first recommendation was that "the likelihood ratio is the preferred approach to mixture interpretation".

To properly apply the Frye standard, it is important to clarify exactly who comprises the "relevant scientific community" in DNA mixture interpretation. I described the forensic scientists who largely focus on DNA inference and statistics. These researchers develop, discuss, publish, validate and assess DNA interpretation methods. In particular, they lay the scientific foundation for forensic practitioners, and may be more engaged in theory than practice.

I showed Judge Martin a 2001 scientific article about DNA mixture interpretation written by the Pennsylvania State Police laboratory in nearby Greensburg. Former laboratory director Christine Tomsey wrote that genotypes can be inferred from the data. Specifically, she approved of using a known contributor's genotype, and of considering peak height information.

A study conducted by the federal government showed that DNA mixture interpretation varies between forensic laboratories. Dr. John Butler of the National Institute of Standards and Technology (NIST) had distributed electronic data from the same DNA mixture to over 50 crime labs. The laboratory analysts' interpretations yielded DNA match statistics ranging from 31,000 (having four zeros after the one) to 213 trillion (14 zeros). This study established that the forensic science community uses different DNA mixture interpretation methods, some of which are more informative than others.

Other forensic groups use TrueAllele methods and systems. I showed Judge Martin a 2008 scientific paper by New Zealander Dr. James Curran about his computer method for resolving two person DNA mixtures. Compared with our TrueAllele approach, his equations share the same key variables, and his program finds genotype solutions in the same probabilistic way. Indeed, I pointed the judge to five different computer systems from around the world that all solve DNA mixtures.

I listed fifteen groups in government, academics and industry that had used the TrueAllele technology. For example, Cybergenetics had re-examined the victim remains DNA data from the World Trade Center disaster, in order to help identify missing people.

I showed the judge pictures of how match statistics changed at each of the 13 tested genetic loci, as the DNA mixture interpretation methods become increasingly more informative. I handed him four bar charts of inferred DNA match locus information for the Dr. Yelenic fingernail evidence.

- The *inclusion* method gave a small amount of information at each locus. Multiplying the 13 locus numbers together gave a product of 13,000.
- Dr. Robin Cotton's *subtraction* method made excellent use of Dr. Yelenic's known victim genotype at two of the loci. Considering those

two larger numbers increased the match product up to 23 million.
- The TrueAllele *addition* method again showed more match information at those two loci (considering the victim genotype), but also at several other loci (due to peak height information). This better use of the data further increased the DNA match statistic to 189 billion.
- None of these methods reached the full match strength of Kevin Foley's own genotype, which would have given a statistic of 875 trillion.

It was visually clear from this succession of pictures that nothing magical was going on. As each interpretation method made better use of the available DNA data, the match statistics increased.

Defense attorney Richard Galloway then conducted his cross-examination.

- He questioned how reliable DNA data could give different statistics. The answer, as I replied, resides in the different interpretation methods applied to the data.
- He asked why the computer did not use thresholds in the same way that people did. I said that since the computer accounts for data uncertainty in a more precise way using mathematics, the machine has no need for a coarser human approximation.
- Mr. Galloway also asked whether TrueAllele had ever been used before in court. I told him that no, it hadn't. The Foley case was the first appearance of TrueAllele (or, indeed, any such computer mixture interpretation) in a criminal

case. But the question before the court was TrueAllele's reliability as the scientific method, not its use elsewhere.

It was now for Judge Martin to decide. If he admitted the evidence, this would be the first time in any trial that a sophisticated computer had ever been used to interpret DNA mixture evidence. An adverse ruling, on the other hand, could slow down for many years TrueAllele's adoption by the criminal justice system, as well as diminish the prosecution's case.

Admissibility

On March 2nd, President Judge Martin issued his opinion on the TrueAllele methodology. He wrote that, "it is recognized that there is more information available which more conservative approaches do not consider. Therefore, it seems logical that the scientific community would work towards including that unused data to arrive at a more accurate finding." Citing materials presented at the hearing, Judge Martin ruled that "based on a review of the evidence, the court finds that Dr. Perlin's methodology is admissible pursuant to the Frye rule and Rule 702." The TrueAllele DNA match results would be heard at the Foley trial.

Trial

The DNA evidence against Kevin Foley was presented on March 12th. Jerrilyn Conway of the FBI testified first, followed by Dr. Robin Cotton. My DNA testimony came last. I had never testified in court before.

Answering prosecutor Krastek's questions, I presented to the jury key points from the Frye hearing.

- There is really only one DNA interpretation principle—infer a genotype objectively from the data, and then match it with a reference genotype.
- Different interpretation methods simply make different use of the same data.
- Better use of the data can yield more identification information.

As Dr. Butler's 2005 NIST study had shown, huge variations in DNA mixture match statistics on the same data are expected. The numbers depend on the method used to interpret the evidence. Our National Institute of Justice (NIJ) study on 40 NIST mixture samples could be used as a calibration to predict a match statistic number, based on interpretation method and contributor DNA amount. The 189 billion TrueAllele statistic for a match between Dr. Yelenic's fingernails and Mr. Foley was predictable, and not in any way unexpected.

Mr. Galloway's cross-examination revisited much of the same Frye hearing terrain. I explained to the jury that the different reported match statistics resulted from how different methods used the data. The defense attorney protested that, with precise methods, the same data should give the same answer.

I replied that when a scientist examines a microscope slide with the naked eye (like the weak "inclusion" method), they can only see so far. Using a magnifying glass (i.e., "subtraction" method) on the same slide, they will see more. And, with a microscope (the computer's "addition" approach) they would see even more. "The information is there," I said. "The question is what is the resolution of the instrument that you are using to make the observation."

"Are you uncomfortable with what the FBI does?" asked Mr. Galloway. "No," I replied. "But if you are a doctor trying to diagnose bacterial disease, sometimes you need a microscope. ... I would be more comfortable using a higher precision instrument to make a diagnosis that might be more informative—same slide, same data—just a more precise approach."

Verdict

On the morning of March 18th, State Trooper Kevin Foley testified in his own defense. That afternoon, the prosecution and the defense made their closing arguments. "John Yelenic provided the most eloquent and poignant evidence in this case," said SDAG Krastek. "He managed to reach out and scratch his assailant," capturing the murderer's DNA under his fingernails. The jury deliberated, and that night convicted Mr. Foley of first-degree murder.

Appeal

Kevin Foley appealed his conviction to the Pennsylvania Superior Court. He claimed that Judge Martin erred in admitting my testimony, suggesting that TrueAllele should have failed the Frye test for "novel" scientific evidence. On March 29, 2011, appearing before an appeals court in Pittsburgh, SDAG William Stoycos referenced three bound volumes of scientific publications, hardcopy printouts of the CD articles introduced at the trial. Foley's lawyers argued that DNA mixture interpretation was unreliable, but Mr. Stoycos explained why TrueAllele was a reliable interpretation system.

Two TrueAllele validation studies had already successfully withstood the scrutiny of scientific peer-review. One study used laboratory-generated DNA samples, and found that quantitative analysis performed by TrueAllele was much more sensitive than qualitative analysis such as that performed by the FBI (Perlin & Sinelnikov, "An information gap in DNA evidence interpretation", PLoS ONE, 2009). Another paper used DNA samples from actual cases and reached similar conclusions (Perlin et al., "Validating TrueAllele DNA mixture interpretation", *Journal of Forensic Sciences*, 2011). This casework study "validated the TrueAllele genetic calculator for DNA mixture interpretation" and found that when "a victim reference was available, the computer was four and a half orders of magnitude more efficacious than human review."

In its December 28, 2011 decision, the Superior Court affirmed Judge Martin's ruling. The court noted that scientific studies of TrueAllele's reliability had been "published in peer-reviewed journals; thus, their contents were reviewed by other scholars in the field." TrueAllele may have been a new system, but the appellate court held that it was not "novel" scientific evidence. On February 15, 2012, the Superior Court published its Foley decision, establishing a statewide TrueAllele precedent throughout the Commonwealth of Pennsylvania.

On January 4, 2013, the Pennsylvania Supreme Court issued a *per curiam* Order denying Foley's petition for allowance of appeal. As a result, the Superior Court's affirmance of Foley's judgment of sentence stands, including its determination that expert testimony regarding DNA match probability calculations in mixed sample

DNA cases which relies upon the TrueAllele methodology is admissible into evidence. The intermediate appellate court's determination is binding precedent throughout the Commonwealth of Pennsylvania.

Impact

Over a hundred TrueAllele reports have been issued in criminal cases, helping both prosecution and defense. I have testified on TrueAllele DNA match statistics in state, federal, military and international trials. The Superior Court Foley precedent has accelerated the introduction of objective TrueAllele technology into Pennsylvania courts for DNA mixture evidence. I have given two continuing legal education (CLE) courses in Pittsburgh about TrueAllele and the Foley case, one at Duquesne University, and the other at the Allegheny County Courthouse for trial attorneys.

The Foley case can be instructive for defense attorneys who encounter DNA evidence that may implicate their client. The initial match statistic to Foley of 13,000 was not overwhelming. But the later computer resolution of the DNA mixture into its component genotypes changed the situation, introducing a more accurate (and much more persuasive) 189 billion statistic. By repeating to the jury over and over again the "millions", "billions" and "trillions" statistics of the different experts, the defense reinforced the large numbers. Once reliable science had established the presence of Kevin Foley's DNA under Dr. Yelenic's fingernails, Foley's adamant denial of contact with the victim became less credible. Perhaps giving some explanation of how an innocent intent had accidently escalated into a fatal consequence might have mitigated the verdict or sentence.

Commonwealth v. Foley was a landmark case in the history of DNA evidence. It was the first time that an advanced statistical computing method for interpreting DNA mixtures was ever:

1. used as evidence for a criminal case;
2. admitted into evidence after an admissibility challenge;
3. introduced as evidence in a trial;
4. upheld as reliable evidence by an appellate court; and
5. established as a statewide precedent.

Dr. John Yelenic was brutally and tragically murdered, but the trial that convicted his killer bequeathed to society a powerful truth-seeking technology for bringing criminals to justice.

Timeline
1995-2007

1995 to 1996
John Yelenic meets Michele Magyar-Kamler
Mary Lois Yelenic (John's mother) dies in May.

1996 to 1997
December, John and Michele marry in Las Vegas.

1997 to 1998
John, Michele and her children Nicole and Nathan move into John's home on S. Spring Street, Blairsville, PA.

1998 to 1999
They purchase a larger home and several properties within the Indiana community.

1999 to 2000
Adoption of an eighteen-month-old baby boy from the Republic of Northern Osetiya, Severnay, Russia, who they name John Jay Yelenic (JJ).

2000 to 2001
The relationship between John and Michele begins to fall apart. A separation is now established. She insists that John move out of the house. He relocates back to Blairsville, PA. She and the children remain at the home in Indiana, PA.

2001 to 2002
While surfing Myspace, she posts her bio and meets up with S. Glosser from Johnstown, PA. They soon become

engaged (while still married to John Yelenic). She and the children move into his home.

2002 to 2003

Michele pushes for more custody of JJ as well as additional support money. Her engagement to S. Glosser ends because Michele would not sign the pre-nuptial agreement that Glosser's mother insisted upon if Michele wanted to marry her son. Michele then contacts John who was just closing the sale of their home on White Farm Road, Indiana. John takes a hundred thousand dollar loss on the price so he is able to sell it quickly. With cash he purchases another home for Michele and the children (at 10 Susan Drive, Indiana, PA.), placing the deed in her name free and clear.

2003 to 2004

Indiana State Police Trooper Earlyman, a crime unit investigator, was assigned to interview Michele due to charges of computer hacking brought forth by a male acquaintance of hers. Trooper Kevin Foley assisted, which is how they met. Months later Foley became her live-in boyfriend (while still married to John Yelenic).

2004 to 2005

A sexual molestation charge is filed against John after a visitation. It happened to be a few months before John wanted to take JJ to Disney World (in Florida) where a dental convention was to take place. Charges were dropped after Judge Hanna of Indiana County interviewed JJ who admitted that his mother told him to say that his father had touched him. After the case was dismissed, the trip was planned. Upon picking up JJ his appearance had changed. Michele had his head shaved, dressed in little girl clothes, and his suitcase full of girls' clothing.

2005 to 2006

By January 2006 John was going forth with the divorce paperwork with his attorney Effie Alexander of Pittsburgh. Meetings between John, Michele, and the attorneys were underway. John had his attorney establish a fund for a private investigator to be used to find out who murdered him in case (during this procedure of filing for a divorce) he should be found dead.

Upon receiving the final Marital Agreement, plans were made with a few relatives to be present to witness his signing it in front of a notary on April 13, 2006, at 3:00 p.m. Before this could happen, however, John Yelenic was found dead on the floor in his home at 233 S. Spring Street by the next-door neighbor's son, Craig Uss.

By 3:35 p.m. April 13, 2006, the Blairsville Police had received a 911 call to Dr. John Yelenic's residence. Cpl. Janelle Lydic of the Blairsville Police Department became the responding officer as well as lead investigator in the soon-to-be-classified homicide case.

2007 to 2008

Contacted Mary Ann Clark (cousin of Dr. Yelenic) to offer to assist family and friends with filming a testimonial of the victim. Series of interviews followed throughout the year.

First vigil was held April 17, 2007, on the front lawn of John's home. Over eighty in attendance. No Michele, Nicole, Nathan or JJ present. A lot of media coverage. By mid-May, a Grand Jury convened at the Federal Building in Pittsburgh. Over one hundred subpoenas were issued. I do know for a fact Michele Magyar-Kamler-Yelenic did testify under oath (the first and last time to date).

The posthumous divorce that Attorney Alexander tried to appeal was denied by Judge Hanna. Reason: one cannot divorce a dead person.

Jack Swint, a Cleveland, Ohio, author of true crime themes contacted Mary Ann to see if he could include the story of John's murder in chapter four of his book *Who Killed Pittsburgh*. I met up with Jack Swint, along with Mary Ann in Monroeville, PA. I interviewed him on film. Upon the release of his book, I was able to contact a television reporter for Channel 4, Jennifer Meile (who had been following up on the case from day one) to also interview Swint, which she did after interviewing me, all of which took place September 24, 2007.

The second week of September, Attorneys Effie Alexander and Sam Riech, both who represented John Yelenic in the past, were set to give their depositions. I interviewed them both on film before the cut-off date.

Arrest

Of Trooper Kevin Foley took place September 27, 2007. I guess our interview on Sept. 24, 2007 was spot on to get things moving. I attended the Attorney General's announcement which took place at the Indiana Courthouse. I filmed the entire process from what lead to the arrest (results of Grand Jury findings) to law enforcement involved with the investigations. Even Chief Hess answered questions from the media.

The preliminary hearing was set for November 7, 2007, before Indiana District Judge Guy Haberl. It lasted almost eight hours with standing-room audience as well as hallways filled with family, friends, students from local colleges, patients of Dr. Yelenic, and reporters. But NO Michele Magyar-Kamler-Yelenic.

Television shows such as *48 Hours* and *20/20* were in constant contact as their field production people attended as well as called during the days and months ahead.

Joyce Cucciado, who was Dr. Yelenic's dental assistant early on in his own practice then with him as he went into partnership with Reilly, was visiting her family in Blairsville over Christmas. Mary Ann asked me if I would like to meet her. I jumped at the opportunity and filmed a very emotional interview. Joyce had been John's assistant for over ten years. She knew and observed all the heartache Michele had put John through over the years. Joyce warned him not to marry her, but as she put it, John was in love with Michele's physical make-up. By the time he got the whole picture, he was in too far to get out.

Author's Documented Investigation 2008 through 2010

To better understand all the components that made this case so intriguing on one hand . . . and a tragic tale on the other.

2008

By January I turned the completed documentary over to Mary Ann Clark. However, by February more interviews were being done by the phone and in person (on film). I also decided to begin to retrace several places where Michele Yelenic resided. All in the attempt to get much more familiar with this *person of mystery*.

Brian Parsely was interviewed in the beginning of February. He was a patient of Dr. Yelenic and the individual who told John about a "hot" girl who worked at Uncle Sudsy's (a deli/beer distributorship) in Indiana on Wayne Avenue. I contacted the owners and interviewed Allen Heath and his wife. They verified the dates Michele Magyar-Kamler worked in their deli/beer distributorship while Betty (Michele's mother) managed the hotel portion of the business (back in 1994).

My next stop was in Johnstown, Pennsylvania, which is located further up the mountains of the Laurel Highlands. I was in search of Arlington Street, in particular 121 where Saul Glosser (who Michele was engaged to while married to John Yelenic in 2002) was said to reside. Locating the stately two-story, red/brown brick house with light-green wood shutters, and cream-colored front door on a green grassy front lawn was very pleasant looking. I panned the house with my camera then walked around to the back which was fenced in and surrounded by large trees. I could visualize Nathan and JJ playing outside. The neighborhood appeared safe. Inside the house, I spotted furniture scattered throughout the living room but no sign of anyone living inside. I even rang the door bell to no avail. I panned the front porch where a large white mail container was located next to the front door. It was about one-third filled with letters and magazines. I noticed one of the top letters was addressed to Douglas Glosser.

    A gentleman across the street was walking toward his car. I approached him asking if Saul Glosser resided at 121 Arlington Street. He stated that Saul did, but he had not been at the house for a while. He informed me that he thought Saul was residing in the Winber area of Johnstown in an apartment building.

    A few days later, I ventured up to Indiana looking for 880 White Farm Road, the home John and Michele purchased in 1998. The home was located in an upscale area of Indiana on a beautiful one and a half acre lot. It was a two-story, brown-frame house. It resembled three to four duplexes side by side in a row. The back of the house was where I was told a hockey rink was built for Nathan to practice in (which was now covered with dirt), a large in-ground pool was still used, and a wooden jungle gym with a play house was still standing. A winding red metal fence surrounded the pool area as well as the back yard decks which extended from the second floor and first floors of the house which appeared like a maze. Overall, the house was lovely with stained glass windows, game rooms, four bedrooms, huge kitchen and eat-in areas. The gentleman who purchased the house from John Yelenic had to repair/replace much of the inner walls and wiring due to the condition the house was found in after Michele moved out in 2002. Windows left opened upon her departure invited squirrels and other small creatures to inhabit the house and do extensive damage, leaving John to take a hundred thousand dollar loss on the selling price. The new owner was a professor at the local college (Indiana University of Pennsylvania) with a large family to fill the house. He and his family would be just the folks John Yelenic would have wanted to live in and enjoy the huge home for years to come. I truly got that feeling as I was given a tour of the home.

While cleaning out the larger of the two furnace rooms, the new owner discovered a seven-inch hunting knife in the wooden eaves. When he heard of the murder of Dr. John Yelenic in 2006, he immediately contacted the Indiana Police Department to report what he had uncovered. However, to his amazement, they never came to the house to view his finding! I filmed it.

By May, Attorney Don Bailey was hired by Mary Ann Clark to represent Dr. John Yelenic in a wrongful death lawsuit filed against Kevin Foley, Michele Yelenic and several troopers of the Indiana State Police in Dauphin County. Based on the premise that the State Police of Indiana **did not** intervene nor stop Trooper Kevin Foley (during work hours) when they witnessed his aggressive outrages, comments, and actions concerning the well-being of Dr. Yelenic over the years. A fourteen page response to the allegations of Michele Yelenic's involvement in the conspiracy was filed in the US District Court in Harrisburg by her attorney, Andrew Barbin from Mechanicsburg, PA.

An interesting conversation I had over the phone was with Dr. Hughes of Indiana, PA. His name was given to me by Mary Ann who knew him as the doctor who took care of JJ's ear infections. He was also the father-in-law of Trooper Brian Bono who just happened to be Kevin Foley's partner at the Indiana State Police Barracks. Dr. Hughes expressed a genuine fondness for Foley. He invited him to his home on a regular basis for dinner. Dr. Hughes had a very extensive knife collection and even stated that he had given Kevin a piece or two. What was so interesting about Dr. Hughes was that he had contacted Mary Ann Clark about phone records he kept under lock and key in a safe at his home that were from Bono's cell phone. Those phone records were compiled during April 2006. He was going to arrange to have his daughter, April Bono (Brian's wife, however separated) meet with Mary Ann and give her a copy. I and Mary Ann tried on several occasions to met up with April, but each time she was a no show. Dr. Hughes and Brian Bono were at odds because Brian would not give April a divorce (together they had a daughter). He stated that April was scared to leave Brian because he was a State Trooper. To this day I don't know if anyone was able to see the phone records. Dr. Hughes stated Brian and Foley were in direct communication the night of the Yelenic murder. Surely, the Attorney General's office was able to obtain them. However, there was never a mention of those records at trial. A few years later (2012), Mary Ann did locate the copy which Dr. Hughes had given to her directly and gave me a copy.

One comment Dr. Hughes made that always had me thinking. I asked him how Kevin could get out of Yelenic's home covered in blood without a trace of it being found. He stated that Brian had a flat bed truck.

Why couldn't Kevin jump onto the flat bed and drive to a car wash and get hosed down on it. There are a lot of car washes from Blairsville to Indiana. That could work because there was no blood found in Foley's SUV. After all they were partners at one time, he stated.

    I took the entire conversation with a grain of salt. Dr. Hughes didn't care for Brian so perhaps he was just trying to draw some attention to him with the phone records. To this day, however, that tale still gives me chills. Foley's clothes, shoes, and knife were *never* found!

    By mid-summer the jury pool was established. However, Attorney Galloway was still uncertain that his client could get an unbiased group because of all the media attention the murder had gotten in the past.

    Wayne Borring had contacted Mary Ann claiming he and his son saw two men dressed in State Police uniforms dig a hole and bury a large black plastic bag. I followed up every lead even that one. I'm thinking this is too good to be true. With camera in hand, we arranged to meet up with Mr. Borring. I contacted a reporter from the *Tribune-Review*, Paul Pierce, who had been reporting on the case from the beginning. Needless to say, the hole that Mr. Borring pointed out was now covered with a mountain of dirt. I mean a mountain! Later we found out that Mr. Borring was angry with the State Police for arresting his son and wanted to get back at them by dreaming up this story. According to Agent Kelly of the Attorney General's office who was assigned to investigate the murder of Dr. Yelenic, he, too, interviewed Mr. Borring. Again, every lead must be investigated.

    George Emigh who was Kevin Foley's supervisor at the Indiana Barracks sat down with myself and Mary Ann at Clark Metal to inform us of the civil suit which he had brought against the Indiana State Police for forcing him into early retirement. Apparently he was falsely accused of a sexual harassment claim that resulted in his demotion and transfer to another county. He, therefore, took an early retirement. He, too, had attorney Don Bailey representing him. One of the reasons he felt he was booted out was because the afternoon Dr. Yelenic's body was found, Emigh wanted to get a warrant to go to 10 Susan Drive, Indiana to have Michele and Foley brought in for questioning. However, his persistence with District Attorney Bob Bell would not merit that action to be taken at that time. It was Emigh's understanding that everyone at the barrack felt that his dislike for Foley was at the root for him pushing to get a warrant to bring Michele and Kevin in. But, in reality, Emigh was doing his job. He may have heard the ranting and raving over Dr. Yelenic or even saw Foley playing with his knife from time to time. Other troopers in the unit also stated those observations (under oath several times).

The summer concluded with a visit to Mary Ann's home by Cpl. Janelle Lydic. I interviewed her (on film) as she told us of her role in the investigation of John Yelenic's homicide. Everything from the call to 233 S. Spring Street on April 13, 2006 to the compiling of all critical materials pertaining to the entire investigation was discussed.

Another interesting person I interviewed several times over the phone was Tracy Hillard. She and her husband Keith (an optometrist in Indiana) were friends of Kevin Foley. They all shared the love of running in local races. Tracy expressed another side of Foley's personality to me. She stated Foley was a regular fixture at her home. He told her of his desire to have a family life like she and Keith had with children. Tracy spoke very fondly of him.

Perhaps she saw through his persona. Foley's twin sister, Karen Peck, who resided in Georgia, communicated with Tracy. Therefore, if anyone knew what made Kevin Foley tick, in my opinion, I would think it might be Tracy. Whom I will add, even though I'm ahead of the story, was the only one who came every day to support Foley during his trial. No one in his family attended so faithfully. His brother James and their mother Gail Foley were present in court for the bail hearing in 2008. However, bail was denied by Judge Martin. I did get James and Gail exiting the courthouse on film that day. Tracy was instrumental in giving me Karen's phone number. I did interview her over the phone when she was home from the weeks she spent away due to her job with Lowes.

With the trial date set for November 9, 2008, and the fall elections in full swing, this time period became very critical to the case because both District Attorney Bob Bell and Attorney General Tom Corbett were up for re-election. Many were counting on Tom Corbett losing. In that case, a new person would be in a position to perhaps further delay Foley's case. After all, it had been scheduled for July 2008 and then changed to November (because his attorney Galloway had changed law firms in October). As fate would have it, District Attorney Bell was defeated and Tom Bianco took his position. Tom Corbett was re-elected to Attorney General for a second term, and it was full steam ahead for the trial to take place March 9, 2009.

Every once in a while I would check the internet and go onto "Topix" to read comments from hundreds of Yelenic murder case followers. Too bad I can't include a sample of the comments because they were up into the thousands. There were followers from all over the country adding into the mix from their distaste for Michele Yelenic to the injustice of law enforcement and everything in between.

Closing out the year I sent Kevin a Christmas card. It was difficult to select one that wasn't too Christmassy. I was instructed by the prison counselor that cards were not to have glitter on them. So I found one that was acceptable and sent it to him. I was always hoping he would respond. But he didn't. So I continue to keep in communications with Gail Foley who was living with her daughter Karen and her family. Gail was always in good spirits and again gave me insights into their family life and her children.

She spoke of her young family living in Massapequa, New York while she and her husband owned and operated a motel. Her Long Island accent made the stories come alive for me. We talked about once a week from November through the end of 2008. When I called one morning in January 2009, she asked me not to call again in a very low voice as if not to let anyone hear the request. Perhaps, Karen thought her mother was giving me too much information. Whatever the reason was, I honored Gail's wishes.

2009

The "Topix" website was abuzz with the upcoming trial. I decided to focus my attention on Massapequa, New York. So I called up to see if anyone remembered the Foley family. As luck would have it, a school teacher's wife recalled the children as her husband's students. James Foley was the boy everyone remembered because he was very outgoing and popular especially in sports. Kevin, on the other hand, was quiet, shy, and reserved as was Karen. Even though they were twins, Kevin was a grade behind. There was also another daughter named Donna whose name didn't come up much in my interviews. One gal named Laura Donaldson, was a classmate of James and sent me photos of Kevin Foley in the fourth and fifth grade. He sure did look shy and small in stature for his age. He wore large glasses at the time and unsmilingly seemed to blend into the class group picture. Laura remembered them moving to Florida due to their father's health. The business was sold to another family to operate. However, she stated, James does return to the Massapequa because he married a gal from the area.

Neil Katz from *48 Hours* (a researcher for the show) was assigned to retain contact with Mary Ann Clark and the group while trying to develop a program around the Yelenic murder. He came to Blairsville, PA to wine and dine us. I handed him numerous names, contact numbers, photos and a copy of the documentary, all in the attempt to help him understand the case in general. But he needed more. The one thing no one ever got—an interview with Michele Magyar-Kamler-Yelenic. Even Foley's sister, Karen Peck, would be considered to make the show for him. Unfortunately, as of this writing, no one has ever gotten that opportunity. I came close when I contacted Michele by phone at her home. She answered and I identified myself. Michele was willing to sit down and tell her side of the story, however she suggested I contact her attorney. If he agreed, she would do it. Of course, for what it was worth, I called Attorney Matthew Budash's office (Michele even gave me the number), left my name and number with the receptionist and never heard from Budash. I even was at the Indiana Courthouse looking up information in county recordings office and walked right up to Budash, introduced myself and asked if I could arrange to interview Michele in his office with him present. He simply heard my request, turned, and left the office. Mary Ann was with me and laughed. *48 Hours*, *Dateline*, or *20/20* all tried but were unsuccessful in their attempts to come up with a program based on the murder. They felt if they didn't have the individual closest to the victim, then it wasn't going to work for them. However, I have watched all three of those shows for years and not every immediate family member is present to comment on the cases presented. The plot was there . . . who gets murdered in their home when the next day they are to sign their divorce papers? That wasn't enough to develop a show around. Adding that the assailant is a state trooper living with the victim's estranged wife? The weapon and clothing were never found. Just enough DNA under the fingernail of a dentist (who has to have trim fingernails because they wear surgical gloves) who was able to reach up and scratch his assailant . . . isn't worthy of a story plot? But just wait there's more.

    Things were heating up during the first week of March. Sunday afternoon, March 1st, Mary Ann called me. She had been notified by Tracy Hillard that Gail Foley had passed away. I remember Gail telling me of the cancer she had and the treatments she was under going back in November. Gail's outlook on life and the tone in her voice was gentle never focusing on health issues. I guess she just wanted to discuss the good times she had with her family and I listened. I only wished that the original trial date back in July 2008 had been left alone because Gail would have been able to attend. Even in November when I was in contact with her she would have taken the chance to make the trip up North in the winter to Pennsylvania from Georgia. I often wonder how Kevin took the news while in the back of his mind the trial of his life was to take center stage. Mary Ann was naturally concerned with Foley being able to travel to Jefferson, Georgia. However, Agent Regis Kelly assured her the trial was going forward.

I arranged to have a sketch artist by the name of Julie Engelmann (with the Indiana Counsel of the Arts) to assist in sketching a few scene during the trial but first I needed Judge Martin's permission. His secretary, Robin, had never had such a request before so we took it slowly. A few days later she called me with the okay as long as none of the jury members were included. With that guideline in mind, Julie completed her sketches, which are included in this book. They were also shown during the evening news broadcast on all three local television channels.

March 9, 2009, at 8:30 a.m. in the Indiana courtroom of Judge Martin, the first day of the trial began. No cameras were permitted, which was again one of the problems *48 Hours*, *20/20*, and *Dateline* had with presenting this case. Pennsylvania does not allow courtroom broadcasting. So I had the next best thing—sketches. The one of Kevin looking up was pretty much the body language he gave out during the entire trial. He never looked around the courtroom nor at the jury. It was straight ahead at the witness seat.

The trial went into the next week and ended on March 18, 2009. The jury was handed the case around 2:30 p.m. Tuesday and the verdict was reached by 10:10 p.m. that evening. Kevin Foley was found guilty of one count of first-degree murder. The media was lined outside of the courthouse, ready to get Mary Ann's reaction. I stood beside her as she expressed her thanks to the justice system which didn't let John Yelenic's murderer go free. There were times she felt it could have been easily swept under the carpet. Justice for John became a reality to his family and friends that cold but peaceful moonlit night.

Sentencing was to take place June 1, 2009 in Judge Martin's courtroom at 8:30 a.m. That was also when the impact statements were going to be read. Over a dozen from John's friends had arrived at Mary Ann's mailbox. I have included many of them in the book. Kevin Foley again sat with his eyes straight ahead. But every once in a while he would turn and look over at the jury box where a small-framed, blond-haired woman sat. I kept getting the feeling she was Karen Peck. Tracy Hillard was present seated in the back of the courtroom. I caught up to Tracy outside and asked if Karen was present. She stated that she wasn't. Michele Yelenic was a no-show, as well as Nicole and Nathan. Where were all Foley's family and friends?

When asked by the Judge Martin if Foley would like to address the court, he declined. So the sentencing took place: life in prison with no parole. Again the media was outside to get reactions from Mary Ann, Attorneys Krastek and Galloway (who stressed he would appeal), Monzo (Galloway's second chair), Chief Hess (Blairsville Police Chief) and a statement from Bruce A. Edwards (President of the State Troopers Association) which was read by their public relations representative (a copy is included).

There was only one last thing to do. I wanted to go up to 10 Susan Drive to see if Michele's car was in the driveway.

Where was she? Mary Ann drove me, my husband Gus, and Dr. Maria up to the house Kevin once lived in with Michele. As we approached the house, to our amazement a red pick-up truck filled with furniture was parked in the driveway. My camera had enough film and battery juice to allow me to film the moment. The basement door was open as Nathan and his friends were moving around inside. I could hear Michele's voice. The next thing we saw were the boys upstairs, staring out at us from one of the bedroom windows. The overall outside of the house appeared run down, in need of paint and new doors. Even the decorative flag that flew over the entrance was worn and ripped. As for the lawn and shrubs, they were overgrown. It was sad because I remembered seeing the house a few years earlier and it was well kept (even that was on film to compare). I guess it was time to move on to greener pastures; we heard on the eastern side of Georgia near Savannah, residing in a gated community.

Kevin Foley's first appeal was denied December 2009. He is now on his second appeal. The civil suit will not be heard until all appeals for Foley have been exhausted. According to the Attorney General's Office and Agent Regis Kelly, this is an ongoing case

2010

I was underway in writing this book and just completing my first draft. By the end of April, out of the blue, Mary Ann called to let me know she was contacted by Nicolina Lanni a field producer for Cineflix Inc. of Toronto, Canada. Ms. Lanni had been searching for cases to be presented on a new program that was created titled *'Cold Blood' Investigative Discovery*. She was very interested in the John Yelenic murder case and was willing to come to Blairsville, Pennsylvania, with a film crew to begin the project. I told Mary Ann this would be an opportunity to get this tragedy out to the mass media in the United States, as well as internationally. Within days, I was contacted by Ms. Lanni—who was informed that I had written a draft—asking me all kinds of questions. I sent her up a copy of the draft as well as sent myself one (never opening it) which was the old copyright fashion since there was not time to send it to the copyright office in Washington, D.C. So at least she had a foundation in understanding the dynamics of the case and all the actors.

By the first week of May, Ms. Lanni and her filming crew descended upon Blairsville. I compiled a list of people who I felt would be best in telling the story, based upon their insights and knowledge of the circumstances around the murder. Calls were made to set up interviews to be filmed at a quaint Bed and Breakfast in Indiana, PA. The project took a week to complete that portion of the show. The remainder, filmed in Canada, focused on docudrama scenes. I wasn't so thrilled about how they went about that (such as the actors used and the way it was set up) but, for the most part, the message was captured. The show was to air on prime time nationwide October 19, 2010, and was carried by the Discovery Channel.

To this day people come up to Mary Ann informing her that they viewed the show and always wondered what happened to Michele. I have investigated numerous homicide cases in my career, but the Dr. John Yelenic case is one I could never let go of. Each time I thought it was at the level of closure, another event would reactivate interest. Mary Ann would call about who she spoke to or someone out of the blue would contact me with a follow-up detail to ponder. Which would, of course, lead to another person to talk with.

2013

WHERE ARE THEY NOW?

Mary Ann Clark: Active in her community and Clark Metal. Grandmother of three (two boys, one girl).

Chief Donald Hess: Criminology instructor at Westmoreland Community College.

Jill Gaston: Employed with the Blairsville Police Department.

Janelle Lydic: Still with law enforcement in some capacity.

Bob Bell: In private practice as a defense attorney in Indiana.

Tom and Melissa Uss: Still residing in Blairsville. Both are employed at a technical school in Indiana.

Craig Uss: Married and a computer systems analyst.

Tom Corbett: The present governor of Pennsylvania.

Anthony Krastek: Still with the Attorney General's office in Pittsburgh, PA.

Regin Kelly: Active investigative agent for the Attorney General's office.

Dennis Vaughn: Married Lisa, both living and working in Worchester, Va.

Margaret McCartin: Married and mother of a baby girl.

Tracy Jacobs: Married and active in law enforcement.

Roberta Mack (Bobbi): A counselor with Intermedia Education.

John Jay Yelenic: Now 13 years old residing with Michele in Savannah, Georgia.
Nathan Kamler: Attending Indiana University of Pennsylvania and residing in Indiana, PA.
Nicole Kamler: Veterinarian assistant residing in Pennsylvania and Georgia.
Michele Yelenic: Residing with JJ Yelenic and Gannon Foley in Savannah, Georgia.
Kevin Foley: Solitary confinement in a 9' x 11' cell somewhere in central Pennsylvania.
John Yelenic: In a 6' x 4' coffin at the Blairsville Cemetery.

What happened to John Yelenic in the early morning hours of April 13, 2006, was a tragedy.
The appointed fiduciaries have been doing their duty processing his seven-figure estate ever since.
Who has been protecting his beloved son JJ over the years (2006-2013)? Have there been wellness checks, reports or photos of his living conditions? If JJ, as heir, has an invested interest in the estate, why aren't the fiduciaries responding to him? After all, JJ is a minor until 2018.

AUTHOR'S FINAL THOUGHTS

On March 18, 2009, at 8:08 p.m., the night of the trial when the future of Kevin Foley was in the hands of twelve jurors, an issue surfaced which brought Attorney Krastek, Agent Kelly, and Cpl. Gardner nervously back into a locked-down courtroom, with Attorneys Galloway and Monzo trailing behind. What brought this reaction about I thought to myself? While sitting on hard benches in the hallway word got out that a juror had requested the definition of "reasonable doubt".

Did the State not provide enough evidence to support their guilty charge based on the DNA found under Dr. Yelenic's fingernails? Where were they going with that request?

My imagination took over as I sat staring into space. What if on that night of April 12, 2006 as John was sleeping away on his couch, he awoke to a familiar face. As they sat and talked the conversation turned hostile, then erupted into physical violence with the aid of a knife to finalize the act. Followed by a quick exit out the door.

Ten minutes later Kevin Foley might have made a visit to John's house, seeing a few lights on and thinking perhaps he is still up. Enters into the house through the back door since it is already unlocked. Sees bloody foot prints on the kitchen floor and the dining room floor, and spattered blood on the walls down the hallway, then hears moaning sounds. As a police officer he's armed with a concealed gun, ready to take action if need be. He goes over to John who is laying still on the floor barely breathing. Foley bends down as John grabs at him out of fear and panic. In a low voice, with his mouth filled with blood, John mumbles out a name. Foley tries to make out his words. John's body then spasms; his hands fly up into the air, resulting in a scratch on Foley's face. Foley's reaction is to rapidly get out of the house, knowing that if he is caught there, he would be the person everyone would suspect of murdering John Yelenic. So he leaves. John was too far gone to call 911 in the moments he was with him.

Could that be what a juror might be thinking? Could someone have visited John prior to Foley? Knew Foley carried a pocket knife. Used a pocket knife to murder John Yelenic? John reaches up out of a bodily reaction, scratching Foley's face.

There was never a knife found nor blood in Foley's car. As for the shoeprints, people knew the brand he wore and it was stated in court that he ordered shoes for a number of co-workers from the same company. When he took the witness stand in his own defense, Foley **never** admitted murdering John Yelenic. So "reasonable doubt" could have been a consideration if one had such a version of what happened that night. What a story that would be.

One other item was brought to my attention by a reader of my manuscript. She stated that John appeared to be a saint. A little too good to be true. Perhaps I got caught up in his persona because I got deeper into the case than I normally do. So I had to step back to address the issue. Looking at all the good things John did for his family, friends, employees, and acquaintances . . . what was John getting out of it? After all he was a big fish in a little pond. He was a young, handsome, single dentist making hundreds of thousands of dollars. In the court transcripts it was stated that many individuals received monetary gifts from him, such as support for business investments, medical expenses, vacations, hockey team support, community sponsorship, home down payments, funds for divorces, legal advice, and so forth. Dr. John Yelenic was indeed a valuable man to know. But there were some who hated the fact that he could be so generous with his money. As Joyce Ciccardo, John's dental assistant, pointed out: on the one hand he was a happy-go-lucky person, but on the other hand his wealth became a powerful magnet. Wealth gave him a measure of security by steering people in his direction, but before he could really sort out the good contacts from the bad . . . his time was up.

Last word:

Civil suit #1:08-cv00689-SHR was filed by Attorney Don Bailey in Middle District of Pennsylvania May 2008 on behalf of Mary Ann Clark, individually and as administratrix for the estate of Dr. John J. Yelenic, naming as defendants Kevin Foley, Michele Yelenic, Brian Bono, James Fry, Daniel Zenisek, Brad Shields, Donna Kirkland, Jeffrey Miller, James Fulmer, and Alison Jacobs.

As of December 19, 2012 Attorney Bailey's career in law could be suspended for five years according to the Pennsylvania Disciplinary Board. They have petitioned to have Attorney Bailey's conduct reviewed due to his accusing numerous federal judges of contriving to ruin his long-standing legal career by dismissing, for political reasons, lawsuits he filed

A ruling on Kevin Foley's appeal was reported by Paul Pierce in the *Tribune-Review* on January 4, 2012, under the headline: Dentist Killer's Guilt Stands. Two appeal experts for Kevin Foley had tried to argue that Judge Martin was incorrect to let the jury hear about the bloody shoeprints discovered near the body of Dr. John Yelenic. They argued that the shoeprints were not clear enough to be able to determine the style, size, or brand. There was a nineteen page response by the Superior Court of Pennsylvania No. 2039 WDA 2009 to their appeal. The appeal was denied and filed on December 28, 2011.

This decision was appealed to the Pennsylvania State Supreme Court. That court responded on January 4, 2013. In one sentence the Court stated "that in the Petition for Allowance of Appeal, is denied." All appeals have now been exhausted. According to Foley's sentence, he will remain incarcerated for the term of his natural life.

I was curious about reaction to this news and contacted Tracy Hillard, a friend of Foley's in Indiana. She hadn't heard from him nor seen him since his trial in 2009. I asked if Michele Yelenic had returned to Indiana. Ms. Hillard responded, "Michele isn't welcomed in this community." What a bold statement of opinion. Perhaps the residents didn't appreciate the black eye this high-profile case gave their town and its law enforcement agencies.

There could another reason why Michele has not returned. Remember back on June 1, 2009 a truck was parked in the driveway of 10 Susan Drive and Nathan and his buddies were loading it up with furniture. That was the morning Foley was being sentenced. It also happened to be the same time that a Simi Valley California finance Company (B.C.H. Home Loan Service) filed a mortgage foreclosure suit against Michele Yelenic in the amount of $180,193.00. The Susan Drive property was paid in full (clear deed) in 2002/2003 when Dr. Yelenic purchased it for Michele upon her return from Johnstown (after her engagement to S. Glosser dissolved). The complaint indicated that the financial company had not received a payment since June 1, 2009. Michelle fled to Savannah, Georgia, with the sons of Dr. Yelenic and Kevin Foley.

I guess one can leave the scene of a crime unscathed.

PHOTO GALLERY 177

John and Michele Yelenic (Jan. 1998)
at the Christian and Missionary Alliance Church of
Blairsville for their marriage ceremony for family and friends
upon their return from Las Vegas.
Photo courtesy of Mary Ann Clark, Executrix of estate

Kevin Foley
Attorney General's Press Release 2007

The crime scene showing tape around the car and
the front of the house.
Courtesy of Mike Baker, Indiana coroner

Kitchen entrance to Dr. John Yelenic's home.
Used by his murderer in April 2006.
Courtesy of author's film

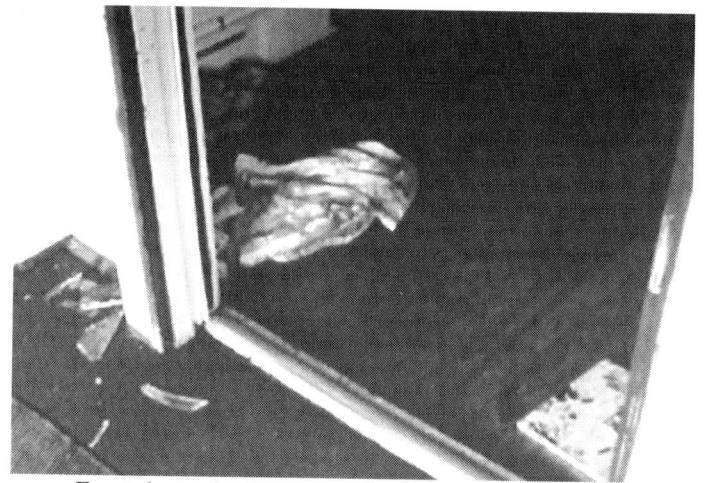

Front door of crime scene, broken glass and blood.
Courtesy of Mike Baker

Front door, inside corner showing bloody walls and rag.
Courtesy of Mike Baker

A group of friends and neighbors gather to pay their respects during the first candlelight vigil on April 17, 2007.
Courtesy of author's film

First candlelight vigil in front of 233 S. Spring St in Blairsville, PA. John Yelenic's college friend, Rev. Mark Woomer officiated
Courtesy of author's film

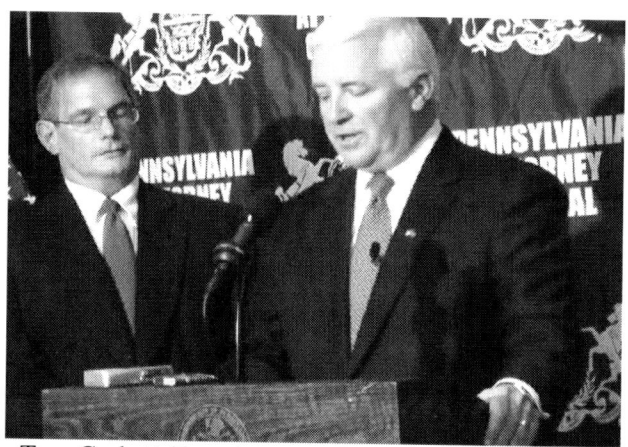

Tom Corbett (then Attorney General of Pennsylvania) announces the arrest of PA State Trooper Kevin Foley for the murder of Dr. John Yelenic.
Indiana County District Attorney Bob Bell is on the left.
Courtesy of author's film

Chief Donald Hess of the Blairsville Police Department.
Courtesy of author's film

Group picture of friends seeking justice for John.
Left to right: Mark Woomer, Mary Ann Clark, Tim Abbey,
Melissa Uss, Craig Uss and Dennis Vaughn.
January 12, 2007
Courtesy of author's film

Dr. John Yelenic's gravesite at Blairsville Cemetery.
Courtesy of author's film

Handout from PA Attorney General's press conference, September 27, 2007

Kevin Foley arriving for the first day of trial, March 9, 2009.
Courtesy of author's film

The trial
Julie Englemann, sketch artist

Defense table. Left to right: Kevin Foley,
Attorney Jeff Monzo and Attorney Richard Galloway.
Julie Englemann, sketch artist

Kevin Foley
Julie Englemann, sketch artist

Richard Galloway, Kevin Foley's defense attorney
Courtesy of author's film

Prosecutor Anthony Krastek
from the PA Attorney General's office
Courtesy of author's film

Forty minutes after Kevin Foley was sentenced on June 1, 2009, a truck is loaded with furniture in the driveway of Michele Yelenic's home.
Courtesy of author's film

Three friends in happier times.
Left to right: John Yelenic, Lisa and Dennis Vaughn.
Courtesy of Dennis Vaughn

APPENDIX

2003 TO 2006

ENTRIES LEADING UP TO DIVORCE

```
1158200822006          Indiana County Prothonotary's Office              Page  2
   PYS835                       Docket Entries                          8/22/2006
   Case No 2003-10944
     MICHELE M YELENIC (VS) JOHN JOSEPH YELENIC
     Date
     Filed
                              - - - FIRST ENTRY - - -

1   6/10/03  COMPLAINT IN DIVORCE
2   6/12/03  ORDER OF COURT DATED JUNE 10, 2003 SETTING A CONCILIATION FOR JULY
             11, 2003 AT 10:30 A.M. IN JURY ROOM 1 FLOOR 4M WILLIAM J MARTIN
             JUDGE COPY TO ATTY
3   6/26/03  ACCEPTANCE OF SERVICE DEFENDANT /MATTHEW L KOVACIK
4   6/15/04  PRAECIPE FOR SUBSTITUTION OF APPEARANCE  OF EFFIE ALEXANDER FOR
             JOHN JOSEPH YELENIC WITHDRAW THE APPEARANCE OF MATTHEW L KOVACIK
             COPY TO ATTY ALEXANDER
5   7/12/04  ANSWER TO COMPLAINT IN DIVORCE AND COUNTERCLAIM
6   7/22/04  ORDER OF COURT INITIAL CUSTODY CONFERENCE AUGUST 27 2004 @ 1:00 PM
             JUDGE MARTIN SIGNED JULY 14 2004 COPY TO ATTY ALEXANDER
7   8/05/04  MOTION TO CONTINUE INITIAL CUSTODY CONFERENCE GENERALLY
8   8/09/04  ORDER OF COURT - CONTINUED GENERALLY  CH   COPY TO ATTY ALEXANDER
9   9/07/04  PETITION FOR SPECIAL RELIEF REGARDING VACATION CUSTODY
10  9/07/04  PETITION TO ESTABLISH INTERIM CUSTODY ORDER
11  9/09/04  ORDER OF COURT - HEARING SET FOR SEPTEMBER 16 2004 @10:00AM COURT
             ROOM #3 FLR 4M COURTHOUSE  CH   COPY TO ATTY ALEXANDER   (TO
             ESTABLISH INTERIM CUSTODY)
12  9/09/04  ORDER OF COURT - HEARING SET FOR SEPTEMBER 16 2004 @10:00AM COURT
             ROOM #3 FLR 4M COURTHOUSE  CH  (SPECIAL RELIEF)
13  9/20/04  INTERIM CONSENT ORDER OF COURT/AGREEMENT REGARDING CUSTODY AND
             VISITATION CAROL HANNA JUDGE COPY TO ATTY
14  9/20/04  ORDER OF COURT   (3) CH   COPIES TO LOVETTE ALEXANDER S BELL
15  9/27/04  EMERGENCY PETITION FOR CONTEMPT AND FOR SPECIAL RELIEF AND TO
             REQUEST COUNSEL FEES
16  10/01/04 ORDER OF COURT - HEARING SET FOR OCTOBER 14 2004 @10:00AM COURTROOM
             #3 FLR 4M  CH   COPY TO ATTY ALEXANDER
17  10/19/04 ORDER OF COURT DATED OCTOBER 14, 2004 CONCERNING AN EMERGENCY
             PETITION FOR CONTEMPT AND FOR SPECIAL RELIEF AND TO REQUEST
             COUNSEL FEES  CAROL HANNA JUDGE COPIES TO ALEXANDER AND LOVETTE
18  10/17/05 AFFIDAVIT UNDER SECTION 3301(D) OF THE DIVORCE CODE DEFENDANT'S
             COPY TO ATTY ALEXANDER
19  10/17/05 AFFIDAVIT OF NON MILITARY SERVICE    COPY TO ATTY ALEXANDER
20  10/27/05 PLAINTIFF'S COUNTER-AFFIDAVIT UNDER SECTION 3301(D) AND 3323(C1) OF
             THE DIVORCE CODE
21  10/26/05 AFFIDAVIT OF SERVICE OF DEFENDANT'S AFFIDAVIT UNDER 3301(D) OF THE
             DIVORCE CODE   (COPY TO ATTY ALEXANDER)
22  10/25/05 PRAECIPE TO WITHDRAW APPEARANCE FOR CUSTODY AND VISITATION -
             DANIEL R LOVETTE ESQ
23  10/25/05 APPEARANCE OF RYAN S FRITZ ON BEHALF OF PLAINTIFF WITH LIMITED
             RESPECT TO CUSTODY AND VISITATION PROCEEDINGS
24  10/28/05 PETITION FOR RETURN OF SEIZED FIREARMS
             11/1/05 JUDGE DID NOT SIGN PETITION IS INCOMPLETE RETURNED TO
             ATTY ALEXANDER
25  10/28/05 PETITION FOR SPECIAL RELIEF TO REQUEST FAMIL COUNSELING
```

```
11582008222006         Indiana County Prothonotary's Office        Page    3
       PYS835                    Docket Entries                    8/22/2006

Case No 2003-10944
     MICHELE M YELENIC (VS) JOHN JOSEPH YELENIC

        Date
        Filed

 26  10/28/05  ORDER OF COURT THE FATHER SHALL BE PERMITTED TO ATTEND FAMILY
               COUNSELING WITH THE PARTIES MINOR CHILD JOHN JOSEPH YELENIC JR THE
               MOTHER SHALL BE REQUIRED TO PARTICIPATE IN SAID COUNSELING IN THE
               EVENT THAT THE COUNSELOR DEEMS PER PARTICIPATION A NECESSARY PART
               OF THE COUNSELING JUDGE HANNA

 27  12/02/05  ORDER OF COURT FOR RETURN OF FIREARMS/AMMUNITION THE FIREARMS
               JOHN J YELENIC SHALLMAKE AN APPOINTMENT WITH THE INDIANA COUNTY
               SHERIFF TO ARRANGE FOR RETURN OF FIREARMS JUDGE HANNA COPY TO
               ATTY ALEXANDER /SHFF

 28   3/20/06  PETITION TO ENFORCE SETTLEMENT AGREEMENT AND TO STAY SUPPORT
               ENFORCEMENT PROCEEDINGS AND FOR COUNSEL FEES ON BEHALF OF DEFENDANT

 29   3/28/06  ORDER OF COURT MARCH 22 2006 HEARING SCHEDULED FOR MAY 18 2006 AT
               1:15 PM  JUDGE HANNA COPY TO ATTY ALEXANDER

 30   4/20/06  VERIFICATION

 31   4/20/06  AFFIDAVIT OF CONSENT - DEFENDANT

 32   4/20/06  AFFIDAVIT OF CONSENT - PLAINTIFF

 33   4/20/06  WAIVER OF NOTICE OF INTENTION TO REQUEST ENTRY OF A DIVORCE DECREE
               PLAINTIFF

 34   4/20/06  WAIVER OF NOTICE OF INTENTION TO REQUEST ENTRY OF A DIVORCE DECREE
               DEFENDANT

 35   4/20/06  PRAECIPE TO TRANSMIT RECORD

 36   5/18/06  ORDER OF COURT CONCERNING AN ORAL MOTION TO DETERMINE THE PARTIES'
               ECONOMIC RIGHTS AND OBLIGATIONS   THE MARRIAGE SETTLEMENT
               AGREEMENT SIGNED BY THE PLFF, MICHELE M YELENIC ON APRIL 7, 2006
               AND CONSENTED TO BY MARY ANN CLARK PERSONAL REPRESENTATIVE FOR THE
               ESTATE OF JOHN JOSEPH YELENIC JR SHALL BE ENFORCED CH JUDGE

 37   6/13/06  BRIEF IN SUPPORT OF MOTION FOR ENTRY OF DECREE IN DIVORCE FILED ON
               BEHALF OF THE ESTATE OF JOHN J YELENIC JR A/K/A JOHN YELENIC JR
               AND ON BEHALF OF ALL PARTIES COPIES TO ATTY ALEXANDER

 38   7/26/06  OPINION AND ORDER OF COURT AND NOW THIS 26TH DAY OF JULY 2006, THIS
               MATTER HAVING COME BEFORE THE COURT ON DEFENDANT'S MOTION FOR
               ENTRY OF DECREE IN DIVORCE, AND AFTER CAREFUL CONSIDERATIN OF THE
               ARGUMENTS IN FAVOR OF THIS MOTION ON BEHALF OF PLAINTIFF AND
               DEFENDANT, IT IS HEREBY ORDERED AND DIRECTED THAT THE MOTION FOR
               THE ENTRY OF A POSTHUMOUS DIVORCE DECREE IS DENIED. CH JUDGE COPIES
               TO BUDASH, D. LOVETTE, E ALEXANDER AND PAUL BELL II

- - - - - - - - - - - - - - - - - LAST ENTRY - - - - - - - - - - - - - - -
```

MARITAL SETTLEMENT AGREEMENT
TO BE SIGNED BY DR. JOHN YELENIC
ON APRIL 13, 2006, AT 3:00 PM
HOWEVER, INSTEAD OF SIGNING THIS, HE WAS FOUND MURDERED THAT DAY.

IN THE COURT OF COMMON PLEAS OF INDIANA COUNTY, PENNSYLVANIA

MICHELE M. YELENIC,

    Plaintiff,

vs.

JOHN JOSEPH YELENIC,

    Defendant.

10944 CD-2003
- IN DIVORCE -

MARITAL SETTLEMENT AGREEMENT

Filed on Behalf of:
BOTH PARTIES

Counsel of Record for Plaintiff:

Daniel R. Lovette, Esquire
PA ID #18140

KAMINSKY, THOMAS, WHARTON & LOVETTE
360 Stonycreek Street
Johnstown, PA 15901
(814) 535-6756

Counsel of Record for Defendant:

Effie G. Alexander, Esquire
PA ID #44719

REICH, ALEXANDER, REISINGER & FARRELL, LLC
Firm #960

1000 Koppers Building
436 Seventh Avenue
Pittsburgh, PA 15219
(412) 391-3700

IN THE COURT OF COMMON PLEAS OF INDIANA COUNTY, PENNSYLVANIA

MICHELE M. YELENIC,	)	
Plaintiff,	)))	10944 CD-2003 - IN DIVORCE -
vs.	))	
JOHN JOSEPH YELENIC,	))	
Defendant.	)	

MARITAL SETTLEMENT AGREEMENT

THIS AGREEMENT, made this _____ day of _____, 2006, by and between **Michele M. Yelenic** (hereinafter "Wife") and **John Joseph Yelenic** (hereinafter "Husband").

Witnesseth

WHEREAS, the parties were married on December 31, 1997, in Las Vegas, Nevada; and

WHEREAS, one child was adopted during the marriage: John Joseph Yelenic, Jr., born June 16, 1998; and

WHEREAS, certain marital disagreements, disputes and unhappy differences have resulted in the filing of a divorce action in the Court of Common Pleas of Indiana County, at Case No. 10944 CD-2003; and

WHEREAS, the parties have been living separate and apart since on or about March 6, 2002; and

WHEREAS, either party may be entitled to support and maintenance in any support proceeding and/or alimony, alimony pendente lite, equitable distribution of marital property, counsel fees, legal costs and expenses and other relief provided for under the Pennsylvania Divorce Code of 1980; and

WHEREAS, it is the desire of the parties, after long and careful consideration, to amicably adjust, compromise and settle all property rights and all rights in, to, or against each other's property or estate, including property heretofore or hereafter acquired by either party, and to settle all disputes existing between them, including any and all claims for maintenance and/or support, alimony and alimony pendente lite, equitable distribution, counsel fees, costs and all other relief provided for under the Divorce Code of 1980; and

WHEREAS, each of the parties has retained or has had the opportunity to retain independent legal counsel of his or her selection, and each has been fully advised or has had the opportunity to be advised by his or her respective attorney of the impact of the Divorce Code; and

WHEREAS, each of the parties acknowledges that he or she has made to the other a full and complete disclosure of their respective assets, estate, liabilities and sources of income, and they waive any specific enumeration thereof for purposes of this Agreement; and

WHEREAS, each of the parties hereto has carefully read and fully understands all the terms, conditions and provisions and the legal effect of this Agreement and believes it to be fair, just, adequate and reasonable as to each of them, and, accordingly, both HUSBAND and WIFE freely and voluntarily accept such terms, conditions and provisions set forth herein.

NOW, THEREFORE, with the foregoing recitals hereinafter incorporated by reference and deemed an essential part hereof, each of the parties hereto, intending to be legally bound hereby, mutually promises, covenants and agrees as follows:

1. The parties shall at all times hereafter live separate and apart, free from any control, restraint, interference or authority, direct or indirect by the other in all respects as fully as if they had never been married.

2. The parties mutually waive any right to take against each other's Last Will under the present or future laws of any jurisdiction whatsoever and each party has a right to dispose of his or her property by Last Will or as he or she may determine, subject to any exceptions set forth herein to the contrary.

3. Husband and Wife do hereby mutually release each other and the estate of the other for all time to come, and for all purposes whatsoever, from any and all rights and claims against the property, income and gain from property and estates of each other, in which either of them now has or hereafter acquires an interest, whether in the nature of dower or courtesy, widow's or widower's rights, family exemption or similar allowance, under the intestate laws, the right to take against the spouse's will, the right to treat a lifetime conveyance by the other as testamentary, or all other rights of a surviving spouse to participate in a deceased spouse's estate, whether arising under the laws of Pennsylvania, any other state, commonwealth or territory, or any other country, except as set forth in this Agreement.

4. The parties further do hereby mutually release each other and the estate of the other for all time to come from any rights which either may have or at any time hereafter have in the nature of equitable distribution or marital property, past, present or future spousal support or maintenance, alimony, alimony pendente lite, counsel fees, costs or expenses, whether arising as a result of the marital relation or otherwise, excepting only all rights and agreements and obligations of whatsoever nature arising or which may arise under this Agreement and/or child support obligations or for the breach of any of the provisions hereof.

5. Except as otherwise provided herein, the parties have divided their personalty, including but not limited to their jewelry, furniture, household belongings, etc., to their mutual satisfaction. Whereupon a full division of personalty and furnishings has been completed, the parties agree and acknowledge that any personalty or belongings shall be titled in the name of the person

having possession of said personalty and the other party hereby waives, releases and abandons any claims with respect to said personal property and/or belongings, which are and shall be the sole and separate property of the other.

6. Except as provided otherwise herein, any property, real or personal, acquired by either party after separation, shall be the sole and separate property of said party, free from any claim of the other party.

7. The parties agree that Wife shall receive the following amounts (in cash) as full and final distribution of all assets, free and clear of any claims by Husband:

a.	For Wife's share of White Farm real estate:	$12,260.00
b.	For Wife's share of Grandview real estate: (see paragraphs 10d & 13)	$14,888.40
c.	For Wife's share of Husband's Dental Practice: (see paragraphs 10a & 16)	$21,000.00
d.	For counsel fees: (see paragraph 26)	$6,000.00
	TOTAL	$54,148.40

The sum of $54,148.40.00 (FIFTY-FOUR THOUSAND ONE HUNDRED FORTY-EIGHT and 40/100 DOLLARS) shall be paid to Wife as follows:

    a. Wife shall receive $34,000.00, which represents the entire balance being held in escrow by Wife's counsel and consisting of the proceeds from the sale of various marital properties/assets.

    b. Husband shall pay to Wife the sum of $20,148.40 in full within ten (10) days of the date this Agreement is signed.

8. Additionally, Wife shall receive the total sum of $38,410.00 (THIRTY-EIGHT THOUSAND FOUR HUNDRED TEN and 00/100 DOLLARS) from Husband's T. Rowe Price annuity for Wife's interest in same and for her interest in the IRAs. Wife's attorney shall prepare

the Domestic Relations Order (DRO) or Qualified Domestic Relations Order (QDRO) or any other instrument necessary to effectuate this provision. Husband shall cooperate fully with regard to same.

9. Any and all debt and/or tax obligations associated with any or all assets received by Wife as a result of equitable distribution shall be the sole responsibility of Wife. Wife shall hold Husband harmless and indemnified as to same.

10. The parties agree that Husband shall receive the following assets, free and clear of any claim by Wife:

  a. Husband's dental practice (see paragraphs 7c & 16);

  b. The balance of Husband's T. Rowe Price annuity, after transferring Wife's share per paragraph 8 above (also see paragraph15);

  c. Hand money from Grandview property.

  d. Grandview property (see paragraphs 7b & 13).

  e. Mahaffey Camp Cottage #143.

11. Any and all debt and/or tax obligations associated with any or all assets received by Husband as a result of equitable distribution shall be the sole responsibility of Husband. Husband shall hold Wife harmless and indemnified as to same.

12. Other than stated above, each party shall receive any and all other assets, tangible or intangible, currently in his/her possession, name, and control.

13. It is acknowledged that Wife has already signed several Deeds, conveying all of her right, title and interest in certain non-marital pieces of real estate to Husband. Husband shall continue to enjoy said real estate, free and clear of any claims by Wife.

14. It is acknowledged that the parties own a joint and marital rental property (4-unit apartment building) located on Grandview Avenue, Indiana, Pennsylvania. This asset shall be transferred to Husband solely and shall become his separate property. Wife shall sign a special

warranty deed conveying all of Wife's interest, right and entitlement of this asset to Husband within ten (10) days of signing this Agreement.

 a. Husband shall be solely responsible for any and all obligations in the nature of loans and/or liens against the home. It is both parties' understanding that there are presently no other liens and/or obligations with respect to the home other than the mortgage with Indiana First. Husband will also be responsible for all obligations including payment of real estate taxes, insurance, repairs, maintenance and utilities for said real estate, and shall indemnify and hold Wife harmless for any amount which he might be called upon to pay as a result of her default of this provision.

 b. Each party represents that he or she has incurred no liabilities, liens or judgments, which encumber the real estate, except for the mortgage set forth above.

 c. Any expenses and costs of the transfer assignment herein of the said property to Husband shall be born solely by Husband.

 d. Husband shall become the sole owner of the existing homeowners' insurance policy(ies) and any and all past, present, and/or future claims thereon and Wife will execute any documents necessary to effectuate this provision.

 e. Husband shall retain the hand money (approximately $2,000.00) relative to the Grandview property currently being held by a third party. (See paragraph 10 c.)

15. Husband shall become the sole owner of the Amertas life insurance policy (#2103172269) insuring his life and shall maintain the parties' son as irrevocable beneficiary until the child reaches age 18, at which time he may designate whomever he chooses as beneficiary of said policy. Husband shall be fully responsible to paying the premiums on this policy.

16. Except as set forth in paragraph 15 above, each party shall become the sole owner of any policy insuring his/her life and shall have the complete right to designate whomever he or she pleases as beneficiary thereof. Additionally, each party shall retain any and all cash value pertaining to their respective life insurance policies.

17. The parties acknowledge that Husband has interest in a T. Rowe Price annuity. It is agreed that Husband will retain any and all of his interest in said annuity (see paragraph 10b) after transferring Wife's share (per paragraph 8), free and clear of any claims by Wife. Furthermore, Husband shall have the complete right to designate whomever he pleases as beneficiary of any and all of his assets, including pension and/or any form of retirement benefits and/or survivor benefits.

18. The parties acknowledge that Husband has a partnership interest through his dental practice, Reilly & Yelenic. It is agreed that Husband will retain any and all of his partnership interest, whether marital and/or non-marital (see paragraph 10a), free and clear of any claims by Wife, and that Wife waives any right, title and/or interest she may have in same, except as otherwise set forth in paragraph 7c above.

19. Any and all other bank accounts (C.D.'s, savings, money market, checking or otherwise), investments and holdings, credit union accounts, and/or retirement plans, whether said plan be an IRA, annuity, 401(k), defined benefit plan or otherwise, personalty, jewelry, and other assets, both tangible and intangible, shall be the sole and separate property of the party whose name the account is currently in, and/or the person who controls and/or possesses the asset, free and clear of any claims by the other party. Each party shall sign any documents necessary to remove their names from any accounts or assets of the other party.

20. Any and all other debts, contracts, obligations or liabilities incurred at any time in the past or future by either of the parties shall be paid solely by the party who incurred such debt, unless and except as otherwise set forth in this Agreement. Each of the parties hereto shall now and at all times hereafter hold harmless and keep the other indemnified as to any debts or liabilities incurred by said party or for which the said party is responsible by virtue of this Agreement.

21. Each party waives any right, title or interest to any and/all future acquired assets and/or all other assets, tangible or intangible, currently in the other party's name and/or possession or control, unless otherwise set forth herein.

22. The parties acknowledge that Wife is currently receiving alimony pendente lite and child support in the amount of $3,875.00 per month pursuant to an Order of Court dated November 29, 2005.

    a. Husband's counsel will prepare a separate PACSES Order to terminate the current Order and replace the existing Order with the agreed upon terms of child support only.

    b. The parties agree to terminate alimony pendente lite effective December 31, 2005, and enter into a separate support Order for $1,337.00 per month as child support only, effective January 1, 2006.

    c. Husband shall provide medical insurance for the minor child and shall be responsible for 100% of the child's unreimbursed medical expenses in excess of the first $250.00 per year, which shall be the sole responsibility of Wife. Wife shall provide Husband with evidence of her payment of the first $250.00 per year prior to Husband being obligated to pay 100% of the remaining balance. Also, Wife must take the minor child to providers that participate in Husband's medical insurance plan for the child.

d. Child support is modifiable in accordance with Pennsylvania law.

23. Beginning in the 2006-2007 school year, Husband will pay the minor child's school tuition at St. Bernard's. Wife shall be fully responsible for the minor child's school uniforms, activity fees, and gym uniforms. For 2005/2006, Husband agrees to pay to Wife directly the additional sum of $200.00 to compensate her for a payment she made to St. Bernard's School for the minor child's 2005/2006 tuition. Additionally, Husband will pay directly to St. Bernard's School the sum of $3,400.00 or whatever amount is due and owing to St. Bernard's for the 2005/2006 school year.

24. The parties agree that Husband shall receive the minor child as an exemption for federal, state, and local purposes until such time as Wife obtains meaningful employment for which she would accrue a federal tax liability, at which time the issue of the exemption shall be discussed and mutually agreed upon by the parties. If necessary, Wife shall timely execute and deliver any and all applicable IRS forms, including Form 8332, so that Husband may claim the exemption.

25. Except as set forth herein, both parties do forever hereby waive, release and relinquish any rights which he or she may have against the other to receive additional alimony pendente lite, alimony, or other spousal maintenance or spousal support.

26. Effective the last day of the month in which a Decree in Divorce is issued, Wife shall maintain her own medical, dental, and vision insurance policies at her own expense and shall be fully responsible for her own unreimbursed medical expenses.

27. Husband agrees to pay $6,000.00 for counsel fees to Wife's attorney within ten (10) days of the signing of this Agreement (these are the same fees also set forth in paragraph 7d). Other than as set forth herein, each party shall be solely responsible for their own counsel fees and expenses with the exception of anything herein to the contrary and/or a court imposing attorney's fees in a contempt proceeding or as a sanction.

28. Any and all rights the parties may have as to custody of their minor children are fully preserved. It is acknowledged that this Agreement does not purport to deal with custody, that custody is modifiable in accordance with Pennsylvania law, regardless of anything herein to the contrary, and that all rights with respect to same are preserved.

29. The parties agree that neither of them shall contest the granting of a mutual consent Divorce Decree pursuant to Section 3301(c) of the Divorce Code of 1980 and each shall promptly execute Affidavits of Consent, Waivers of Notice, and other documents necessary to obtain a Decree within five (5) days of the date of this Agreement, if they have not already done so prior to that date.

30. It is further agreed, covenanted and stipulated that this Agreement, or the essential parts hereof, shall be incorporated, but not merged, in the parties' Decree in Divorce, which will be issued by this Court, for the limited purpose of enforcement of the contractual obligations of the parties pursuant to the relevant provisions of the Divorce Decree. This Agreement shall not be merged in the parties' Decree but shall in all respects survive the same and any related Order and be forever binding and conclusive upon the parties. The parties agree and intend that said incorporation is for the purpose of enforcement only, and not to vest in the Court issuing the Decree in Divorce any power to modify the terms of the Agreement, unless specifically stated to the contrary herein. As provided for in §3105 of the Divorce Code, this Agreement shall be enforceable by the Court where the Decree in Divorce is obtained.

31. A modification or waiver of any of the provisions of this Agreement shall be effective only if made in writing and executed with the same formality as this Agreement. The failure of either party to insist upon strict performance of any of the provisions of this Agreement shall not be construed as a waiver of any subsequent default of the same or similar nature.

32. It is specifically understood and agreed by and between the parties hereto that each party accepts the provisions herein made in full settlement and satisfaction of any and all said parties' right against the other for any present and future claims on account of spousal support and maintenance, alimony, alimony pendente lite, counsel fees, costs and expenses, retirement and pension rights, life insurance, equitable distribution of marital property and all other claims of each party, including but not limited to all claims raised by them or potential claims that could have been raised in the divorce action pending between the parties or which have arisen out of the parties' marriage, separation and divorce, with the exception of child support and/or related obligations.

This Agreement shall constitute a final document resolving any and all parties' respective claims past, present, and future, except as may otherwise specifically be provided hereunder.

33. It is expressly stipulated that if either party fails in the due performance of any of his or her material obligations under this Agreement, the other party shall have the right, at his or her election, to sue for damages for breach thereof, to sue for specific performance, to seek any other legal remedies as may be available, and the defaulting party shall reimburse the non-defaulting party his or her counsel fees, costs and expenses incurred by the non-defaulting party in any action or proceeding to compel performance hereunder.

34. Husband and Wife each acknowledge that the other party has fully disclosed the following to him or her: the nature and extent of all property in which each party had an interest as of the execution of this Agreement; the nature and extent of all liabilities that each party had as of the execution of this Agreement; and the nature and extent of all income that each party had as of the execution of this Agreement. Husband and Wife each acknowledge that he or she is fully aware of the right to engage in discovery by any means of discovery permitted by the Pennsylvania Divorce Code or the Pennsylvania Rules of Civil Procedure. In this regard, Husband and Wife acknowledge that they each have provided the other with all documents and information that the other may have requested and that each has waived his or her respective rights to conduct additional discovery. Husband has retained the services of Effie G. Alexander, Esquire, and Reich, Alexander, Reisinger &

Farrell, LLC, to represent him in connection with these proceedings. Husband has retained the services of Daniel R. Lovette, Esquire, and Kaminsky, Thomas, Wharton & Lovette to represent her in these divorce proceedings.

35. If any term, condition, clause or provision of this Agreement shall be determined to be void or invalid at law, or for any other reason, then only that term condition, clause or provision shall be stricken from this Agreement as is held to be void or invalid, and in all other respects, this Agreement shall remain in full force and effect.

36. This Agreement shall be forever binding and conclusive on the parties; and shall not be subject to modification by this Court, unless specified to the contrary herein. Any modification of this Agreement must be in writing signed by both parties and executed with the formality of this Agreement.

37. In the event of the death of either party before his/her obligations to the other with respect to the transfer of their respective interests in any assets and/or any other transfer or conveyance required under this Agreement have been fully discharged, any obligations undertaken by each in the within Agreement shall be binding upon their heirs, executors, administrators, and assigns of each, and shall constitute a charge against his/her estate, unless set forth to the contrary herein.

38. Each party shall promptly execute any and all documents necessary to effectuate the terms and conditions of this Agreement.

39. No provision of this Agreement shall be interpreted for or against any party because that party or that party's representative drafted this Agreement in whole or in part. In the construction of this Agreement, the parties hereto intend and agree that the separate provisions of this Agreement shall be construed as a whole and, where possible, consistent with each other.

40. All matters affecting the interpretation of this Agreement and the rights of the parties hereto shall be governed by the laws of the Commonwealth of Pennsylvania.

41. This Agreement constitutes the entire understanding of the parties and supersedes all prior agreements and negotiations between them. There are no representations or warranties other than those expressly set forth herein.

42. All other claims of the parties are hereby dismissed, except as specified in this Agreement.

WITNESS: AGREED and CONSENTED TO:

_____ _____
                              Michele M. Yelenic

_____ _____
                              John Joseph Yelenic

ACKNOWLEDGEMENT

On this _____ day of _____, 2006, before me, a Notary Public, the undersigned officer, personally appeared John Joseph Yelenic, known to me (or satisfactorily proven) to be the person whose name is subscribed to the within instrument and acknowledged that he executed the same for the purposes therein contained.

IN WITNESS WHEREOF, I hereunto set my hand and official seal.

_____
Notary Public

My Commission Expires

ACKNOWLEDGEMENT

On this _____ day of _____, 2006, before me, a Notary Public, the undersigned officer, personally appeared Michele M. Yelenic, known to me (or satisfactorily proven) to be the person whose name is subscribed to the within instrument and acknowledged that she executed the same for the purposes therein contained.

IN WITNESS WHEREOF, I hereunto set my hand and official seal.

_____
Notary Public

My Commission Expires

CRIME REPORT
APRIL 13, 2006

BLAIRSVILLE BOROUGH POLICE DEPARTMENT

Page: 1	Case No: 06-001650	
Beat:	Rpt Dist:	Type: Investigation Ongoing	Seq: 1

Crime / Incident (Primary, Secondary, Tertiary): **1 HOMICIDE** 2501

Attempt	Occurred	Date	Time	Day
	On or From	04/13/2006	15:25	Thu
	To	04/13/2006		Thu
	Reported	04/13/2006	15:25	Thu

Location of Incident: 233 S SPRING ST, BLAIRSVILLE, PA
Cross Street: W. SOUTH ALLEY

County: **INDIAN**

V — Last, First, Middle: **YELENIC, JOHN J**
- Race: W, Sex: M, Age: 39, HT: 509, WT: 185, Hair: BRO, Eyes: BLU
- Home Phone: (724) 459-7713
- Address: 233 S SPRING ST
- DOB: 02/20/1967
- City, State, Zip: BLAIRSVILLE BOROUGH PA 15717
- SSN: 178-48-1658
- State: PA

RP — Last, First, Middle: **JENNINGS, TOM**
- Sex: M, Age: 62, HT: 0, WT: 0
- Home Phone: (724) 459-7403
- Address: 453 S LIBERTY ST
- DOB: 03/09/1944
- Work Phone: (724)
- City, State, Zip: BLAIRSVILLE PA 15717

Synopsis:

UCR: 01A
Gang Related: N
Pursuit:
Disposition: **PEND**

Assigned To: **OFFICER JANELLE LYDIC** Date: 04/17/2006
Officer ID: OFFICER JANELLE LYDIC 3603
Reviewed By: **OFFICER JILL GASTON** Date: 04/17/2006

CRIME SCENE LOG

BLAIRSVILLE BOROUGH POLICE DEPARTMENT 1 E MARKET STREET BLAIRSVILLE, PA 15717	Page 1	**Incident Supplement Page**	
	Case No.	**06-001650**	
	Reported 04/15/2006	14:00	Saturday

Title: *Patrolman Brant's (crime scene log)*

Log of persons at crime scene (233 S. Spring street, Blairsville borough)

1539 hrs - Patrolman John Brant called to 233 S. Spring street by Patrolman Isherwood and Corporal Janelle Lydic.

1600 hrs - Deputy Coroner, Jack Edmundson arrives on scene.

1607 hrs - District Attorney, Robert Bell arrives on scene.

1613 hrs - Blairsville Fire Dept. closes the 200 block of S. Spring street to vehicle and pedestrian traffic.

1619 hrs - Indiana County Coroner, Mike Baker and Deputy Coroner, Chuck Conrad arrive on scene (unit 660).

1621 hrs - Patrolman McCully arrives on scene.

1634 hrs - Patrolman McCully is given the shoes of Craig Uss voluntarily (Craig did step in house).

1636 hrs - Patrolman McCully is given the shoes of Zachary Uss (Zachary did not step in house).

1645 hrs - Chief Don Hess arrives on scene.

1652 hrs - Jeff Whitmeyer notified to assist in investigation by Robert Bell and PSP Sergeant, George Emigh.

1700 hrs - County Detective Frank Stanley and Dave Rostis arrive on scene.

1710 hrs - Patrolman Brain Murphy arrives on scene.

1722 hrs - PSP R&I unit arrives on scene, Troopers Brian Kendgia and Chuck Gonglik.

1726 hrs - Blairsville police intern, Frank Sebastianelli arrives on scene.

1729 hrs - Trooper Kendgia, Gonglik and Mike Baker enter the residence.

1730 hrs - Patrolman Brian Mutchler arrives on scene and is posted at the rear of the residence in the alley to secure perimeter.

1740 hrs - Patrolman Jill Gaston arrives on scene.

1743 hrs - Troopers Kendgia, Gonglik and Mike Baker exit the residence.

Officer ID		Agency	Reviewed By	Date
OFFICER JOHN BRANT	3605	BLVS	OFFICER JILL GASTON	04/17/2006

BLAIRSVILLE BOROUGH POLICE DEPARTMENT	Page 2	Incident Supplement Page
1 E MARKET STREET, BLAIRSVILLE, PA 15717	Case No.	06-001650
	Reported	04/15/2006 14:00 Saturday

Title: *Patrolman Brant's (crime scene log)*

1745 hrs- Detective Whitmeyer arrives on scene.

1750 hrs- Trooper Kendgia and Gonglik enter residence again to look at crime scene.

1820 hrs- Fire Chief, Dan Durilla, Chief Hess and Robert Bell walk to the bottom of the steps of residence to talk about covering the porch with tarp due to oncoming rain.

1823 hrs- Dan Durilla, Chief Hess and Robert Bell exit the porch area.

1824 hrs- Fire Department begin to cover back porch with tarp due to rain. Patrolman Steve McCully, Dan Durillia, George Berkley, Donna Lenhart and Jim Meighan on the ground securing tarp. Tom Barbarich and Terry Sherpard are on the porch roof to secure tarp.

1832 hrs- finished covering back porch all persons leave the perimeter.

1834 hrs- Fire Department begin to cover front porch, Tom Barbarich and Jim Meighan are on the porch roof. Patrolman McCully, Dan Durillia, Donna Lenhart and Jim Meighan are on the ground to secure tarp.

1841 hrs- Front porch is covered by tarp, all parties leave the perimeter.

1914 hrs- PSP Greensburg trooper, Tiko Angellechio arrives on scene and looks inside residence.

1916 hrs- Donna Lenhart, Tom Barbarich, Jim Meighan put additional wood bloocks on the tarp on the ground to help secure it.

1918 hrs- Above people finished securing the tarp and leave area.

1928 hrs- Trooper Angellechio leaves the residence.

1952 hrs- PSP Greensburg trooper, Lori Bernard arrives on scene.

2003 hrs- Corporal Janelle Lydic brings mailman into yard to look at the front door.

2005 hrs- Corporal Lydic and mailman leave the area.

2009 hrs- Detective Whitmeyer leaves the scene for the night.

2040 hrs- Patrolman McCully, Tom Barbarich and Donna Lenhart remove cribbing (wood) from tarp.

107 hrs- Patrolman Brant and Corporal Lydic enter residence to start to collect additional evidence. Troopers Gonglik and Kendgia are still inside the residence and are finished with processing the scene.

Officer ID OFFICER JOHN BRANT	3605	Agency BLVS	Reviewed By OFFICER JILL GASTON	Date 04/17/2006

BLAIRSVILLE BOROUGH POLICE DEPARTMENT 1 E MARKET STREET BLAIRSVILLE, PA 15717	Page 3	**Incident Supplement Page**	
		Case No. **06-001650**	
		Reported 04/15/2006 14:00 Saturday	

Title: Patrolman Brant's (crime scene log)

2111 hrs- Trooper Angellechio and Bernard enter the residence to assist Blairsville officers on search for additional evidence.

2129 hrs- Attic/ playroom appears normal, windows unlocked but appear normal.

2134 hrs- Bedroom/ 1 window locked and 1 unlocked, but appears normal.

2200 hrs- both children's room appear normal, windows unlocked, but appear normal. Upstairs bathroom appears normal.

2320 hrs- Finished checking the residence for additional evidence. 1 digital camera taken (by Blairsville PD). from living where body was found, Camera was sitting on a end table beside the couch. A camcorder was also taken into evidence that was on a stand near the television along with numerous tapes for the camcorder. Also a safe was taken from the basement as evidence.

2340 hrs- Troopers Gonglik and Kendgia are finished for the night and leave.

0030 hrs- Fire Department, Tom Barbarich and Dan Durillia secure front entrance by fastening plywood over the door. All remaining persons leave for the night.

Officer ID: **OFFICER JOHN BRANT**	3605	Agency **BLVS**	Reviewed By **OFFICER JILL GASTON**	Date **04/17/2006**

REPORT BY OFFICER JILL GASTON

On Thursday 4-13-2006 at approx. 2330hrs **_Deputy Coroner Chuck Conrad_** and I arrived at 10 Susan Ave Indiana Borough, residence of **_Kevin Foley_** and **_Michelle Yelenic_**. **_Michelle_** is the considered the next of kin to deceased **_John Yelenic_**. The residence is a two story family dwelling with a driveway to the left of the house. We pulled up to the front of the residence and the upstairs front two corner windows had lights on. There was 2 vehicles parked in the driveway.

Deputy Coroner Conrad rang the doorbell and then knocked several times with the end of his mag light. We received no response, the house was not marked with a number therefore we went to a neighbors residence 12 Susan Ave, which had lights on and the front door was open and a dog was in the yard. The neighbor lady confirmed the house we were at was indeed the residence of **_Kevin_** and **_Michelle_**.

Deputy Coroner Conrad and I went back to the residence and rang the doorbell and knocked several times again at which time a light on the inside turned on and **_Kevin_** came to the door. **_Deputy Coroner Conrad_** introduced us and asked if **_Michelle Yelenic_** was home and **_Kevin_** advised she was in bed and he would get her and **_Kevin_** asked us in, **_Michelle_** was standing at the top of the steps when we entered. **_Conrad_** asked if she was **_Michelle_** and he introduced us again and asked if we could go to the kitchen to speak. When we entered the Kitchen and the light was turned on I noticed **_Kevin_** had an approx 1 inch long scratch which was red and "swollen" the mark was above his left eye. **_Michelle_** advised that she heard that **_John_** had died. **_Conrad_** walked into the Kitchen and stood in front of **_Michelle_** who sat down in a chair at the kitchen table, she sat at the edge of the chair with her arms crossed. **_Kevin_** stood to the right of the entrance way and I then stood to the left to have a view of both **_Kevin_** and **_Michelle_**.

Conrad asked **_Michelle_** what she had heard she first looked up at **_Kevin_** whom gave her an affirmative nod, she then looked at **_Conrad_** and then looked down and advised that "she received a call from **_John's_** cousins the **_Swazy's_** whom she remained friends with and that they advised they heard over the radio and seen the fire company at **_John's_** house and that **_John_** had died of a heart attack." **_Conrad_** advised that **_John_** indeed had passed and that the death is suspicious and that the Blairsville Police are investigating the case. He gave her his business card and advised if they needed anything anytime to call, questions regarding funeral arraignments or anything. **_Conrad_** then asked if she had any questions she first looked up at **_Kevin_** whom gave her a negative nod, she then looked at **_Conrad_** and then looked down and advised "No". **_Kevin_** then turned to me and asked "who is handling this you guys" I advised yes along with the District Attorneys Detectives and the Greensburg State Police. They thanked us for coming and we left.

LOCAL REGISTRAR'S CERTIFICATION OF DEATH

COMMONWEALTH OF PENNSYLVANIA
DEPARTMENT OF HEALTH VITAL RECORDS

WARNING: IT IS ILLEGAL TO ALTER THIS COPY OR TO DUPLICATE BY PHOTOSTAT OR PHOTOGRAPH.

CERT. NO. T 6008811

Date of Issue of This Certification: APR 16 2006

Name of Decedent: John (First) ___ (Middle) Yelenic, Jr. (Last)
Sex: Male
Social Security No.: 178-48-1658
Date of Death: Found: April 13, 2006
Date of Birth: February 20, 1967
Birthplace: Latrobe, PA
Place of Death: 233 South Spring Street (Facility Name), Indiana (County), Blairsville (City, Borough or Township), Pennsylvania
Race: White
Occupation: Dentist
Armed Forces? (Yes or No): No
Marital Status: Divorced
Decedent's Mailing Address: 233 South Spring Street (Number, Street), Blairsville (City or Town), PA (State)
Informant: Maryann Clark
Funeral Director: Richard L. Shoemaker
Name and Address of Funeral Establishment: Shoemaker Funeral Home Inc, 49 N. Walnut Street, Blairsville, PA 15717

Part I: Immediate Cause | Interval Between Onset and Death
(a) Exsanguination | minutes
(b) Lacerations of Head, Neck, Chest and Right Arm
(c)
(d)

Part II: Other Significant Conditions: Mult. Superficial Lacerations

Manner of Death:
- Natural ☐
- Accident ☐
- Suicide ☐
- Homicide ☑
- Pending Investigation ☐
- Could not be Determined ☐

Describe how injury occurred: Decedent was assaulted in his home

Name and Title of Certifier: Michael A. Baker - Coroner (M.D., D.O., Coroner, M.E.)
Address: 249 Chestnut Street, Indiana, PA 15701

This is to certify that the information here given is correctly copied from an original certificate of death duly filed with me as Local Registrar. The original certificate will be forwarded to the State Vital Records Office for permanent filing.

Catherine Delioco   32-290 (District No.)
Local Registrar of Vital Records
310 Patton Avenue, Blairsville, PA 15717

April 16, 2006 — Date Received by Local Registrar

NOTE: "DIVORCED" LISTED FOR MARITAL STATUS

INTERVIEW 4-20-2006 WITH DENNIS VAUGHN

POLICE DEPARTMENT
01 E MARKET STREET
ILAIRSVILLE, PA 15717

Case No: **06-001650**
Reported: 04/20/2006 16:00 Thursday

T̲ : Lydic Interview with Dennis Vaughn

Dennis Vaughn called and scheduled a time to come into the station to speak with us. Mr. Vaughn and his girlfriend Lisa Marple stayed at Dr. Yelenics residence Saturday Night. They stated that following;
*Dennis Vaughn is a Psychologist
*Lisa Marple works in the hospital collections department.
*The 2 of them live in the same household.
*They arrived on April 8, 2006 around 1300 hrs.
*Mr. Vaughn came due to a tooth problem.
*They drove Ms. Marple's vehicle a white toyota Forunner
*They stayed in Dr. Yelenic's residence and watched some movies with him and talked.
*They then got ready and went to the Ironwood ar in Indiana and met up with a friend Richard Palermo from Ruby Tuesdays that Dr. Yelenic was talking about.
*They left Ironwood around 10:30 -11:00 pm and went to Drillers in Indiana.
*@ Drillers he met a girl he went out with and John got very drunk.
*John drinks Blue Moons.
*House was unlocked while they were gone.
*Doesn't remember if the back door was locked
*John had a very "spartin" Life style
*John always bought when they would go out.
*Sunday April 9, 2006 around 11am Dr. Yelenic and Mr. Vaughn went to the office on E. Market street to look at Mr. Vaughn's tooth.
* ̲ ile there Dr. Yelenic found an unknown male working on the computers.
*John was angry of finding this male stating that it was a patient or former patient of Dr. Reilly's and he is only there to check on the records to breech the contract between Dr. Yelenic and Dr. Reilly. Dr. Yelenic stated that he was collating data and also stated "I can't believe Tom is doing this". The agreement was that if Dr. Reilly would leave he would only get $48,000.00 as per the buy out clause in the contract.
*Dr. Yelenic and Dr. Reilly got along "ok".
*Dr. Reilly was getting nervous about his retirement.
*Dr. Yelenic stated "I don't know if I am going to confront Tom or not".
*Dr. Yelenic stated that he is not going to budge on the contract between them.
*A picture was in the picture album on the coffee table in the living room of a female in Pittsburgh during there super bowl trip. The female is married and the picture is of the female and John together. She is married and her husband was there. She gave John a business card and he sent her a picture of them together the week prior to this incident.
*Mr. Vaughn and Ms. Marple also stated that there is a picture of Michele in the Photo album. They stated that this is out of place because Dr. Yelenic stated that this album had pictures of the past year. Michele's picture was when Dr. Yelenic first met Michele.
*Dr. Yelenic said that when the divorce is over, he was going for custody of Jay because he is tired of going thru Trooper.
*Dr. Yelenic would give Michele money if she wanted it.
*Dr. Yelenic stopped giving her muney recently and said no more.
* ̲ Yelenic gave money to alot of people including a Tim Abbey for a down payment on his house.

Officer ID		Agency	Reviewed By	Date
OFFICER JANELLE LYDIC	3603	BLVS		/ /

POLICE DEPARTMENT 201 E MARKET STREET BLAIRSVILLE, PA 15717	Case No. **06-001650** Reported *04/20/2006* 16:00 Thursday

Title: Lydic Interview with Dennis Vaughn

No One had a problem. Everyone loved him.
* Dr. Yelenic was on Lexapro (anti-depressant) he took himself off of it about 1 month ago.

When asked what could have happened to him they both said Michele and Trooper.

| Officer ID: OFFICER JANELLE LYDIC 3603 | Agency: BLVS | Reviewed By: | Date: / / |

IN THE COURT OF COMMON PLEAS
ALLEGHENY COUNTY, PENNSYLVANIA

IN RE:	:	SUPREME COURT OF PENNSYLVANIA
	:	149 W.D. MISC. DKT. 1998
THE TWENTY-SIXTH STATEWIDE	:	
	:	ALLEGHENY COUNTY COMMON PLEAS
INVESTIGATING GRAND JURY	:	NO. 1182 M.D. 1998
	:	
	:	NOTICE NO. 19

TO THE HONORABLE BARRY F. FEUDALE, Supervising Judge:

PRESENTMENT NO.

    We, the Twenty-Sixth Statewide Investigating Grand Jury, duly charged to inquire into offenses against the criminal laws of the Commonwealth, have obtained knowledge of such matters from witnesses sworn by the Court and testifying before us. We find reasonable grounds to believe that various violations of the criminal laws have occurred. So finding with not fewer than twelve concurring, we do hereby make this Presentment to the Court.

                                                        _____

                                                        Foreperson - The Twenty-Sixth Statewide
                                                        Investigating Grand Jury

DATED: _____, 2007

INTRODUCTION

We, the members of the Twenty-Sixth Statewide Investigating Grand Jury, have received and reviewed evidence pertaining to an investigation of the murder of Dr. John Yelenic. This investigation was conducted pursuant to Notice of Submission of Investigation Number 19 and, by this Presentment, this Grand Jury hereby makes the following findings of fact and recommendation of charges:

FINDINGS OF FACT

In May, 2007, the Twenty-Sixth Statewide Investigating Grand Jury began receiving testimony regarding the murder of Dr. John Yelenic.

Pennsylvania State Police Corporal Randall Gardner testified that on Thursday, April 13, 2006, at approximately 3:25 p.m., the body of John J. Yelenic, D.M.D., was discovered in the living room of his home located at 233 South Spring St. within the Borough of Blairsville, Indiana County, PA. Dr. Yelenic was a white male approximately six foot two inches tall, he weighed approximately 225 pounds. The initial responding investigators observed that the living room and adjacent foyer were extremely bloody. Blood smears, in addition to pools of blood, indicated that a struggle had taken place. A glass side light window which is situated beside the front door of the residence was found by investigators to be broken. Blood was observed on and around the broken window. Broken glass was also observed on the floor of the foyer area of the residence as well as on the floor of the front porch of the residence. The associated curtain and two curtain rods were observed to be bent, twisted, off its mounting hooks and blood soaked. The curtain itself was on the floor in the foyer. The Victim's body was found in the living room area of the residence near another large pool of suspected blood. Suspected blood was observed on the walls and furniture within the residence located in the foyer, hallway and living room.

Cpl. Gardner further testified that because of the obvious indications of a struggle, it would be reasonable to conclude that there was physical contact between the victim and his assailant that could lead to the transfer of evidence from the actor to the scene and/or victim as well as from the scene and/or victim to the actor. The force used could have possibly resulted in injury to the actor.

The victim was barefoot. Several bloody shoe prints/impressions were discovered at the scene, beginning near the victim's final resting place in the living room area of the residence and continuing from the living room, through the dining room and kitchen and out of the residence through a rear door. The bloody shoe prints/impressions were photographed and/or collected. Photographs and CD images of the bloody shoeprints/impressions, along with evidence found inside the victim's residence with bloody shoeprints/impressions, were sent to an FBI lab for testing in August and September, 2006. A Report of Examination from the FBI laboratory indicates that these bloody shoe prints/impressions "most closely correspond with laboratory reference materials for an ASICS 'Gel Creed' or 'Gel Creed Plus' shoes". The FBI examiners further consulted with a Mr. Brice NEWTON of the ASICS America Corporation and determined the impressions measure between size 10 through 12 ½ men's shoe.

The victim was pronounced dead at the scene by the Indiana County Coroner's Office at approximately 4:10 p.m.

On Friday, April 14, 2006, an autopsy was performed on the body of John Yelenic by Dr. Cyril H. Wecht. The final opinion reached by Dr. Wecht in his report was the following: "This autopsy illustrates an instance of death in a 39 year old white male due to exsanguination (blood loss) as a result of multiple, extensive lacerated wounds of the scalp, face, neck, trunk, and right arm. Deep wounds through the thyroid and cricoid cartilages are noted with bleeding into the tracheobronchial tree. No significant ante mortem disease processes are noted. The manner of death is homicide." Most of the lacerated wounds, according to Dr. Wecht, were consistent with slashing knife wounds.

Biological samples were also taken from the victim at the time of autopsy, which included fingernail clippings and a blood sample.

Cpl. Gardner testified about interviews conducted by Pennsylvania State Police Investigators of the individuals residing near the Dr. Yelenic's residence. According to Gardner, five neighbors recalled hearing unusual noises in the early morning hours of April 13, 2006 coming from the vicinity of the victims' residence and described variously as males arguing, blood curdling screams or noises like pig squeals. Some neighbors were awakened by dog barking. These five neighborhood witnesses approximated the time that they heard this disturbance as between 1 a.m. and 2 a.m. on April 13, 2006.

On December 31, 1997 John Yelenic married Michele Magyar-Kamler. The couple adopted a child, J.J. Yelenic, on March 17, 2000. The two separated on March 6, 2002. Michele Yelenic filed a Complaint in Divorce against the Victim on June 10, 2003. Michele Yelenic and/or their juvenile, adoptive son would be the beneficiary to the victim's estate and life insurance benefits that amount to more than 1 million dollars.

The divorce proceedings between John and Michele Yelenic had become extremely heated, involving the police on more than one occasion. The victim was forced to spend countless hours of time and thousands of dollars in legal expenses defending against allegations that he physically and sexually abused his adoptive son. All of these allegations were subsequently determined to be unfounded. Michele Yelenic made increasing demands for money from Dr. Yelenic. It was learned through the victims' attorney, Effie Alexander, that the victim had always given into the financial demands of Michele Yelenic throughout their separation. It was only in the last days of the victim's life that he had begun to resist his ex-wife's financial demands. According to Alexander, this infuriated Michele Yelenic.

According to the employees at the Victim's dental practice, Michele Yelenic called the victim at the practice continuously and demanded money. Within days of the murder and for the first time, the Victim refused to take Michele Yelenic's calls.

Georgette Johnson testified that she worked as a receptionist for Dr. Yelenic, beginning in 2004. Johnson testified that Michele Yelenic called frequently, asking to speak to Dr. Yelenic. Dr. Yelenic always took those calls prior to April, 2006. On April 3 or 4, 2006, Dr. Yelenic refused to take a call from Michele Yelenic. Michele Yelenic told Johnson that she wanted money from an escrow account to pay some bills for J.J. Yelenic. Still refusing to take the call, Dr. Yelenic had Johnson tell Michele Yelenic to get in touch with her lawyer and that if she signed the divorce papers, he would giver her the money. Michele Yelenic continued to insist to Johnson that she needed money from Dr. Yelenic, that she would have to get food stamps for their son, and that she intended to go "to the media" with her complaint. The divorce settlement would have decreased Michele Yelenic's monthly support check from the victim by

—4—

approximately $2,500. The support would have changed from approximately $3,800.00 to approximately $1,300.00 per month. Nevertheless, in the event of Dr. Yelenic's death, J.J. Yelenic would become the sole beneficiary of Dr. Yelenic's estate. Michele Yelenic would then be J.J. Yelenic's sole remaining parent and caretaker.

Michele Yelenic testified that Kevin Foley moved into her residence at 10 Susan Drive, Indiana PA at the end of 2004. Her three children, including J.J. Yelenic, lived with them from that time.

Kevin Foley is a Pennsylvania State Trooper stationed at Pennsylvania State Police Barracks in Hollidaysburg. At the time of this incident, Foley had been assigned to the Criminal Investigation Unit at the Pennsylvania State Police Barracks in Indiana. Duties associated with that assignment would include the investigation and prosecution of criminal acts ranging from Criminal Mischief to Criminal Homicide.

According to Cpl. Gardner, Foley has received training and education in the law enforcement field. Foley has been a United States Army Military Policeman, holds a Bachelor of Arts Degree in Criminology from the University of South Florida, and has completed the Pennsylvania Municipal Police Officers Training Academy (Act 120). Foley enlisted in the Pennsylvania State Police in 1994 and has received continued law enforcement training. Some of the training Foley has completed as a Pennsylvania State Police Trooper includes the following, Interview and Interrogation, Testifying in Court, Crime Scene Protection and Evidence Collection, Advanced Crime Scene Investigation, Search and Seizure, along with numerous other training classes. Foley was also a designated Department Physical Fitness Coordinator since 2001 and received associated training in that field as well. Foley has therefore attended training and has been exposed to procedures involving the detection, collection and preservation of evidence.

Kevin Foley's enmity towards Dr. Yelenic was often and passionately stated. Trooper Kirkland testified that she was working with Kevin Foley on March 28 or 29, 2006, just two weeks before the Yelenic murder. They were on a prisoner transport, driving to Westmoreland County, and Foley said he "wished that Dr. Yelenic would die or be killed in a car accident." Kirkland cautioned Foley that his comment was inappropriate. According to Kirkland, Foley replied, "I know, but I'm so frustrated, you know, with everything." Kirkland testified that Foley told her he "prayed" that Yelenic would die. Kirkland said this was not the first time Foley told her he prayed for Yelenic's death. In a previous conversation at the barracks, according to Kirkland, Foley said he told his mother that he prayed that Yelenic "would just die." When Kirkland suggested he shouldn't say that, Foley responded, "I just can't help it."

Pennsylvania State Police Trooper Daniel Zenisek worked with Kevin Foley at the Indiana barracks. According to Zenisek, Foley's expressions of ill-will toward Dr. Yelenic were "pretty much a daily thing." Zenisek testified, "He (Foley) never said a good thing (about Yelenic). It was just every day, this and that, you know, he is this, he is that. He is a child molester, a piece of shit. It got to the point where, hey, Kevin how you doing, I hate this guy, you know."

On one occasion, Foley was disparaging Yelenic in the PSP patrol room. According to Zenisek, Foley "said he would like to kill the cocksucker" and asked Zenisek if he would like to help. At the time, Zenisek said he did not take the comment seriously; however, he added, "He (Foley) had an extremely deep hatred for the man (Yelenic)."

Pennsylvania State Police troopers who worked with Foley testified that he habitually played with knives. Trooper James Fry testified that Foley "seemed to enjoy the knife... I mean, it was not uncommon to see him walking up the hall to you, you know, and he just had that knife out, flicking it open, you know, open/close, open/close, open/close, open/close. Even at roll call, he sits over there and open/close, open/close, open/close. It wasn't uncommon." Fry recalled an incident where Foley was, as usual, "flicking that knife around" and cut Fry's pants in the groin area. Fry testified, "He like, come up, flicked it open, and like slashed it back and forth. But I mean, it caught me right in the groin, and I jumped back."

Trooper Daniel Zenisek corroborated Fry's testimony about Foley's fascination with knives. Zenisek testified, "He (Foley) would just pull it out, flip it around, screw with his fingernails. He was always fiddling it. I don't know if it was a nervous habit or what, but he was always fiddling with it... Just always playing with that knife, liked to play with that knife."

Both Fry and Zenisek noticed that after Dr. Yelenic was murdered, Foley stopped playing with his knife. Fry recalled Foley playing with his knife as late as April, 2006, but "after the homicide, I never once recall seeing him with the knife, with the knife out, or playing with the knife." Zenisek testified, likewise, that he never saw Foley playing with a knife after Yelenic's body was found.

Evidence collected by the Grand Jury also established that Foley, who repeatedly expressed his hatred of Dr. Yelenic, drove near the victim's house near the time the murder occurred. Foley played in an ice hockey game at the

Center Ice Arena located off S.R. 22 in Salem Township near Delmont, PA on April 12, 2006. He arrived at the hockey arena at approximately 10:30 p.m. He played in the hockey game and left the arena at approximately midnight. A number of other participants in the hockey game were interviewed by Pennsylvania State Police Investigators and did not observe Foley with any injuries. None of the other participants at the game knew of anyone receiving any injuries during the game.

At the time of Dr. Yelenic's murder, Foley owned and operated a two-tone red Ford Explorer with tan-colored trim which outlined the vehicles wheel wells and the bottom of the vehicle. Foley resided just outside of Indiana Borough in Indiana County. The most expedient route of travel from the Center Ice Arena to Indiana would be to travel east on S.R. 22 after leaving The Center Ice Arena and then travel north on S.R. 119 to Indiana. S.R. 22 travels through the municipality of New Alexandria, PA. Surveillance video from a business in New Alexandria, PA depicts a vehicle resembling that owned by FOLEY at the time traveling east on S.R. 22 at approximately 12:18 a.m. on April 13th. Surveillance video of a business in Blairsville borough located at the corners of Walnut and Market Streets depicts a vehicle resembling the Ford Explorer owned by Foley traveling north on Walnut Street and then turning east onto Market Street at approximately 1:48 a.m. on April 13, 2006. This is within the period of time when Dr. Yelenic's neighbors heard the disturbance coming from the vicinity of the Victims residence.

The vehicle depicted on the surveillance video from the Blairsville business would have been traveling from a location in the vicinity of the Victims' residence as described above. The path the vehicle, depicted on the surveillance video from the Blairsville business, was traveling was in the direction of S.R. 119.

Foley was observed to have an injury above his left eye after the murder of Dr. Yelenic. Blairsville police officer Jill Gaston accompanied the Indiana County Deputy Coroner to Foley's home the night of April 13, 2006. Officer Gaston testified, "Above his (Foley's) left eye was, approximately, a one-inch long gash that was red and swollen, and then there was another little scratch below the left eye." She described Foley's wound as "fairly fresh." Foley's fellow troopers also observed this injury to Foley's face the day Dr. Yelenic's body was discovered. Trooper Deana Kirkland, who worked with Foley on a daily basis, testified that she did not see any injury to Foley's face on April 12, 2006. On April 13, 2006, however, she saw an abrasion above Foley's left eyebrow. Trooper Robert Worcester, who played hockey with Foley on April 12, 2006, testified he saw no injury to Foley when they left, separately, after the game. The next day, Worcester noticed a one to two inch scratch on Foley's face. Worcester testified, "It was above, I believe, his left eye. It was like a half-moon, half-circle, maybe like above the nose over the eyebrow."

A search of the Foley/Yelenic residence was conducted by Pennsylvania State Police investigators on October 11, 2006. A hockey equipment gear bag was seized in that search and secured in the secure evidence holding facility located at the Pennsylvania State Police Barracks in Greensburg PA.

Kevin Foley was served a Pennsylvania Investigating Grand Jury subpoena on June 8, 2007 requiring him to produce any and all hockey equipment bags in Foley's possession at the time of Dr. Yelenic's murder. Foley's response, through his legal counsel, was that the Pennsylvania State Police already had his hockey bag.

A co-worker of Kevin Foley's who is stationed at the Pennsylvania State Police Indiana Barracks has been interviewed regarding the hockey bag of Kevin Foley. This individual advised that he used to play hockey and has since quit playing due to time constraints. He advised that when he quit playing hockey Foley approached him and asked if he could purchase his hockey equipment. This individual agreed and did sell most of his hockey equipment to Kevin Foley, including a hockey equipment bag. This individual also indicated that he could absolutely recognize the bag he sold to Kevin Foley because of the individual additions he had made to the bag. On May 10, 2007 this individual was shown the hockey bag secured in evidence at the Pennsylvania State Police barracks in Greensburg. This individual, without hesitation, indicated that the bag in evidence was not the bag he had sold Kevin Foley.

Pennsylvania State Police Corporal Gardner learned through his investigation that Foley was an avid runner and wore ASICS running shoes. Additionally, it has been discovered through investigation that Kevin Foley purchased running shoes directly from ASICS for himself and others, taking advantage of a discount offered by ASICS to individuals in law enforcement. Pennsylvania State Police Investigators also discovered that an order was placed to ASICS by Kevin Foley on August 12, 2003 for a pair of Gel-Creed TN217 running shoes, size 10. That particular style of ASICS had been discontinued. In accordance with ASICS company policy, a pair of ASICS Gel-Creed Plus TN327, size 10 running shoes, were shipped to Kevin Foley on 08/18/03 from the ASICS Company.

Pennsylvania State Police Trooper Allison Jacobs testified that she is a friend and co-worker with Kevin Foley. They shared an interest in running and

ASICS Gel Creed

The above pictured shoe is the ASICS Gel Creed. The shoe was manufactured in various forms between the years of 2002 and 2004. In June of 2004 the ASICS Gel Creed was discontinued and replaced with the ASICS Gel Empire. During the course of time between June 2004 and the present the ASICS Gel Empire has turned into the Gel Empire 2 which is pictured on the attached page.

Shoeprint left by the murderer on dining room floor. It was identified as being the same type of shoe shown above.

Courtesy of author's film

trained together. She testified that Foley wore ASICS running shoes.

Pennsylvania State Police Trooper Daniel Zenisek testified that Foley always wore ASICS. "Everybody gets to know each other's habits, who liked Ford trucks, what kind of beer they drink," according to Zenisek. "[H]e wore ASICS suits and sneakers." Zenisek testified that he knew Foley from 1996 and that "[p]retty much that time I knew him to wear ASICS." After the murder of Dr. Yelenic, however, Zenisek noticed that Foley began wearing NIKE running shoes.

Pennsylvania State Police investigators submitted the fingernail clippings obtained from the victim at the time of autopsy to The Federal Bureau of Investigation Laboratory Division for DNA analysis. A Report of Examination, filed by FBI DNA analyst Jerrilyn M. Conway on September 11, 2007 explaining her findings, was read to the Grand Jury. In particular, Conway found that an examination of the right fingernail yielded the presence of DNA from more than one individual. The DNA profiles of Dr. Yelenic and Kevin Foley could not be excluded as potential contributors to this mixture. Based on the applicable typing results, the probability of selecting an unrelated individual at random from a general population is approximately 1 in 42,000 from the African-American population, 1 in 13,000 in the Caucasian population, 1 in 16,000 from the Southeastern-Hispanic population, and 1 in 28,000 from the Southwestern-Hispanic population. Importantly, the DNA profiles from Dr. Yelenic and Kevin Foley can account for all of the typing results obtained from the specimen examined from Dr. Yelenic's right fingernail.

The Victims' Divorce attorney informed investigators that the Victim had offered to pay her money to fund an investigation in the event that he was found dead. He had expressed to his attorney that he was sure that his estranged wife, Michele Yelenic was going to have her boyfriend, Kevin Foley, kill him. The victim wanted his attorney to investigate his murder due to the fact that Michele Yelenic's boyfriend, Kevin Foley, was a Pennsylvania State Trooper. The victim felt that because of Kevin Foley's influence, his murder would be covered up.

RECOMMENDATION OF CHARGES

Based on the evidence we have obtained and considered, which establishes a *prima facie* case, we, the members of the Twenty-Sixth Statewide Investigating Grand Jury recommend that the Attorney General, or his designee, institute criminal proceedings against Kevin Foley and charge him with the listed offense:

Criminal Homicide – 18 Pa. C.S.A. § 2501.

PRESS RELEASE
www.attorneygeneral.gov
FOR IMMEDIATE RELEASE

CONTACT: Shonna M. Clark
Assistant Press Secretary
717-787-5211 (Cell) 717-418-3774
sclark@attorneygeneral.gov

Thursday, September 27, 2007

Attorney General Corbett announces homicide charges against PA State Trooper in Indiana County murder case

INDIANA – A Pennsylvania State Trooper was arrested today and charged with the 2006 murder of a prominent Indiana County dentist, John J. Yelenic.

Attorney General Tom Corbett identified the defendant as Kevin Foley, 42, of 10 Susan Dr., Indiana.

Corbett, along with Indiana County District Attorney Robert Bell and Pennsylvania State Police officers, announced the charges during a news conference this afternoon at the Indiana County Courthouse.

Corbett said the April 13, 2006 homicide of Dr. John J. Yelenic, 39, was placed before a statewide investigating grand jury in May 2007. The grand jury found evidence linking Foley to Dr. Yelenic's murder.

"It is extremely difficult to have to arrest a member of the law enforcement community, but as in any case, we follow the evidence wherever it leads," Corbett said.

-more-

"State Police worked side by side with the Attorney General's Office and the Indiana County District Attorney's Office in this investigation," said State Police Commissioner Jeffrey B. Miller. "It is a sad day for the Pennsylvania State Police when one of our members is arrested. But everyone, no matter what his or her position in society, must be held accountable for their actions."

The Dr. John J. Yelenic homicide

Corbett said the grand jury found that Dr. John J. Yelenic was killed in the early morning hours of April 13, 2006. Yelenic's body was discovered in the living room of his home located at 233 South Spring St., located within the Borough of Blairsville, Indiana County.

Corbett said that Yelenic died after receiving multiple laceration wounds, most of which were consistent with slashing knife wounds. An autopsy found that the cause of death was exsanguination, or blood loss, as a result of lacerated wounds of the scalp, face, neck, trunk, and right arm.

According to the grand jury, blood pools and smears in various locations inside the residence – including on the walls and furniture located in the foyer, hallway, and living room – indicated that a struggle had taken place. A window next to the front door was broken and blood was observed on and around the window. The window curtain and two curtain rods were bent, twisted off mounting hooks, and soaked in blood lying on the floor in the foyer.

Because the crime scene indicated that a struggle had taken place, a blood sample and fingernail clippings were obtained from Dr. Yelenic and sent to an FBI lab for DNA analysis.

-more-

Corbett said Foley played in an ice hockey game at the Center Ice Arena off route 22 in Salem Township on April 12, 2006. Foley was seen arriving at the ice arena at approximately 10:30 p.m. He played in the hockey game and left the ice arena at approximately midnight.

The grand jury also revealed that when Foley left the arena he did not have any apparent injuries. Following the murder of Dr. Yelenic on April 13, 2006, Foley was observed with a fresh, one-to-two inch gash that appeared to be red and swollen above his left eye. Another small scratch was seen below the left eye.

Corbett said Dr. Yelenic was found barefoot; however, bloody shoe prints were also discovered at the crime scene. Investigators sent photographs and CD images of the prints to the FBI lab, where tests indicated the prints were from an ASICS 'Gel Creed" or 'Gel Creed Plus" shoes, size 10 through 12-and-a-half.

The grand jury revealed that Foley was regularly seen wearing ASICS running shoes and would purchase shoes directly from ASICS through a discount program offered by the company to individuals in law enforcement.

On Aug. 12, 2003, an order was placed to ASICS by Foley for a pair of Gel-Creed TN217 running shoes, size 10. However, the company had discontinued that style, and instead shipped a pair of ASICS Gel-Creed Plus TN327 running shoes, size 10 to Trooper Foley on Aug. 18, 2003.

The grand jury stated that after the murder of Yelenic, Foley was observed wearing only NIKE running shoes.

Corbett said surveillance video taken from two businesses indicates that a vehicle matching Foley's was near Yelenic's home within the time frame that the murder occurred.

-more-

Corbett said the grand jury found that Foley had a well-known hatred for Dr. Yelenic. Foley had been having a romantic relationship with Yelenic's estranged wife, Michele. For more than three years, Yelenic and his wife had been going through a bitter divorce.

Corbett said that at the end of 2004, Foley moved into Michele Yelenic's residence on Susan Drive, Indiana, with her three children, including Dr. Yelenic and Michele's adopted son.

According to the grand jury, Foley publicly stated how he "wished that Dr. Yelenic would die." On one occasion, Foley allegedly asked another state trooper if he would like to help him kill Dr. Yelenic, although the trooper did not take the comment seriously at the time. Foley's comments regarding his hatred for Dr. Yelenic were allegedly a daily occurrence.

Additionally, the grand jury found that it was not uncommon for Foley to be seen playing with a knife. It was revealed that Foley was always opening, closing, and flipping his knife. However, after Yelenic's murder, Foley was never observed playing with his knife again.

Foley enlisted in the State Police on Jan. 3, 1994, and graduated from the State Police Academy on June 24, 1994. He was assigned to Troop A, Indiana, where he has served since that time.

Foley was arrested today and charged with criminal homicide for the murder of Dr. John J. Yelenic.

Foley was arraigned before Indiana County President Judge William J. Martin. He will be prosecuted in Indiana County by Senior Deputy Attorney General Anthony Krastek and District Attorney Bell.

Corbett thanked District Attorney Bell's Office, the Pennsylvania State Police, and local law enforcement for their assistance in this investigation.

-more-

-5-

(A person charged with a crime is presumed innocent until proven guilty.)

###

EDITOR'S NOTE: A copy of the court documents and a photo of the defendant are available by contacting the Attorney General's Press Office at 717-787-5211.

DR. YELENIC MURDER INVESTIGATION
INDIANA COUNTY

KEVIN **FOLEY**

TOM CORBETT
ATTORNEY GENERAL

ROBERT BELL
INDIANA COUNTY
DISTRICT ATTORNEY

PENNSYLVANIA STATE POLICE

Handout from Attorney General's press conference
September 27, 2007

THE FOLLOWING ARE CO-VICTIM IMPACT STATEMENTS READ TO JUDGE MARTIN ON JUNE 1, 2009, BEFORE THE SENTENCING OF KEVIN FOLEY

The Honorable Judge Martin

The April 13, 2006 murder of Dr. John Yelenic by Kevin Foley has caused my family and I emotional trauma and tremendous stress and has forever changed our lives as we knew them.

John Yelenic and I met on the first day of dental school at the University of Pittsburgh School of Dental Medicine in August of 1989. We immediately became friends. John was an only child who always wanted siblings and we became part of each others families in no time. We shared the difficult times of getting through school, the fun times and we stayed dear friends after school ended. We would call each other regularly and visit often even though we lived three hours from each other.

It was early morning Good Friday when the call came. I was in the shower and my husband told me to come out now. He looked at me and said "John." He didn't need to say another word. My first feeling was "Oh my God, they killed him." I sat down on the bathroom floor in a towel and began sobbing and praying "Please God, no!" My children, ages 6 and 5 at the time, came in to see what was wrong. I told them that "Uncle John has become an angel and went to live with God." My oldest child said with tear-filled eyes "You mean Mommy that Uncle John's wife and the bad Trooper killed him?"

My children knew of the hate John's wife and Kevin Foley had for John Yelenic. They did not learn this from John or I. Instead, they heard about it from John's son. Whatever negative feelings John had during the divorce, he never once expressed them in front of his son in our presence. The child would tell my kids that his mommy hates his daddy. When he was angry he said 'Trooper is going to be my new dad and take care of you." John's child was being used a pawn in a game of manipulation and hatred and it was evident even to other young children.

The motto of the Pennsylvania State Police is "To seek justice, preserve peace and improve the quality of life for all." Kevin Foley did the extreme opposite. He made his own form of justice, gave John no peace and disrupted every aspect of his life. He used his ability to manipulate the system while enjoying the protection of the legal system and he intimated and emotionally battered John. This became increasingly evident when my family, John and his son went to Walt Disney World for what John called "the vacation of a lifetime." After switching the youth's school's without John's knowledge and taking him to court to try and prevent him from taking his son to Disney, it was very clear that this trip was not something his child's mother wanted to happen. She made that obvious by not sending him to school the day we were leaving as agreed upon. John had to go to the house to get him and waited over an hour and a half in the car for him to be brought out. When John arrived at our house, the boy's head was shaved. John was shaking. He said Foley said "This isn't over." During the trip John was afraid to discipline his son because he knew that his child's mother and Kevin were looking for any reason to get back at him. Several times during the trip John would have his son call his mom. When he got off the phone he was a different child, filled with anger and rage often hitting and kicking my children. It was difficult to watch John having to deal with this. However, John never lost his temper or raised a hand to the child. A vacation that was suppose to be fun and relaxed was shadowed with anxiety for John.

Shortly after our return from Florida, the real abuse of power began. When John's wife could not convince the Blairsville Police Department that John had physically abused Jay-Jay, Kevin Foley had his fellow officers at the Indiana State Police barracks file those charges. Then a violation of a Protection from Abuse order supposedly happened which resulted in John being led out of his office for all of Blairsville to see and read about. John was cleared, yes cleared, of any wrong doing. His wife and Kevin Foley would not stop there. Next they had the child lie about sexual abuse and once more charges were filed. They broke John's heart having his son lie about such a sick atrocious thing when all he wanted to do was be with his son and love him. However, once again John was cleared of all misconduct but not before being humiliated and denied time with his son. Kevin Foley robbed John of his sleep, caused him psychological pain by abusing his power as a law enforcement official to keep John's son away from him. He denied him precious months with his son while he was alive. Foley kept John's son from him on holidays he could never get back or in time, would never have again. What kind of persons try to turn a son against his father, a father whose entire world was that child? Kevin Foley did that to John Yelenic for months without end. I watched my dear friend have his heart torn apart piece by piece and slowly watched his spirit start to die. It was heart-wrenching.

But it was not nearly as heart-breaking as the moment when Kevin Foley choose to slaughter John like an animal! This loving, humorous, generous, spiritual man suffered an unspeakable death by a person paid and sworn to protect others even to the forfeiture of his own life. Instead, Foley killed John in the most ghastly way imaginable.

This crime has affected my children on many different levels. They do not feel safe around any State Police officers, even if they are their classmates' fathers. They feel you can not go to the State Police for help because they will hurt you. For many months after, they cried at night and asked God why He couldn't protect Uncle John? They often ask how will John's son live without his dad? They worry that something horrible will happen to their father or I. They were forced into an adult's world by this diabolic person, Kevin Foley. He robbed them of some of their innocence of youth and took from them an Uncle they loved very much.

Sometimes I have to remind myself to breath and tell myself that things are okay. This "new normal" is very different from the old normal. Unfortunately, I have experienced the loss of close family and friends before and after this. None has impacted me more than John's death. The nature in which he died haunts my thoughts. I find that my memories become transfixed on his body lying there rather than the happy times we shared. I wonder what John was feeling at the time of the crime and how much pain and suffering he endured? I imagine the fear he felt as Foley was smashing his head through the door and cutting his throat? I lie awake at night and wonder exactly how many minutes John would have remained conscious and felt pain? The guilt and the questions always follow. Would it have made a difference if someone called for help? Why didn't I do something more? The last time I spoke with John he told me "When they have me killed….." I begged him that we go to the Blairsville Police Department and plead for help but he refused saying it would do no good.. John felt powerless against Foley and the State Police. He warned me not to do anything on my own because Foley and his friends were ruthless. Why didn't I just go ahead and do something? Why didn't

Foley's superiors at the barracks see the pattern that was going on and stop him? I believe whole-heartedly that this death could have been prevented if one person stepped up and did the right thing!

I have been in counseling since John's death. People tell me that I need to get on with my own life and I try everyday. They don't understand exactly how hard this is. John knew my husband and I were getting divorced. He always added humor to even the worst of situations and he could always make me feel better. Now my "big brother" wasn't there. Many times I picked up the phone to call him and had to face the harsh reality that he is gone all over again. Part of the divorce agreement was me leaving our joint practice and finding another office to practice dentistry. This was extremely hard when I would start crying when I had time alone. Something in the office would remind me of something we did together in dental school or that we would complain or joke about and the tears just come out. Work was very difficult for along time and there still are moments when I have to compose myself.

One of the hardest things to cope with is trying to have a sense of why John died, why Kevin Foley did this to him? Because it was Easter time when John was murdered, I dread Easter. I can not be in Church when the Passion of Christ is read. The first time I heard it after the homicide, I began to cry uncontrollably in Mass. My mind goes to Kevin slicing John's throat. I use to attend Holy week services consistently. It literally now takes all of my strength on Easter morning to walk in the Church doors.

When I hear of a violent death in my community, I become fixated on the victim and their family. Did the killer realize the victim was a human being? What gives a person the right to take away someone's life - the life of a child, parent, sibling, friend, community leader? It always takes me back to John's murder

My views of law enforcement especially the Pennsylvania State Police have changed drastically. I have a difficult time looking at a State Trooper without wondering why didn't any of them have the guts or morals to report what was happening. I have lost respect for this organization and feel that a Congressional hearing into internal corruption is most necessary. Only after those involved in trying to hinder this investigation are behind bars, will the answers we seek be given and the Blue Code of Silence broken. No citizen should be above the law!

If I lived each day in anger and despair it would only destroy my life. I get through one moment at a time, one day at a time. Nothing will bring John back to those of us who loved him so dearly or to his son. You Honor, Kevin Foley took that away from all of us. He should **NEVER** be put in a position where he could harm another human being. He deserves to spend the rest of his life in the most secure maximum security prison there is. He does not deserve any leniency or mercy. We need to be able to live our lives without fear!!

Kevin Foley's abuse of power to torture John while he was alive was heartless, malicious, and illegal. His butchering John to death is something he should spend the rest of his life thinking about and being haunted by his actions. The justice system turned a blind eye and failed John Yelenic while he was alive. May it not fail him in death by giving Kevin Foley life without parole in the harshest prison possible!

Respectfully,

Dr. Maria J. Tacelosky
Dr. Maria J. Tacelosky

Statement for Foley Sentencing Hearing
Margaret S. McCartin

Your Honor, Ladies and Gentlemen of the court, Mr. Krastic, Mr. Galloway, Mr. Monzo and Mr. Foley,

First of all, to Mr. Krastic, Special Agent Regis Kelly, I want to thank you for all your hard work and never giving up on this case or us. There was a time when I never thought we would be here and I think it's because of your hard work and determination that we are here. We know we weren't always the easiest group to get a long with, but we did it out of love for our dear friend and brother. I think you all came to understand and respect that and it has meant so much to us.

For those of you in local and state law enforcement, particularly Chief Hess who stood up to do the right thing despite the road blocks and political red tape, I thank you.

For those of you who intervened to get this case stopped or blocked its progress, and you know who you are, I hope you face harsh consequences within the confines of the law.

I would like to tell you that I am relieved and happy to be standing here with the opportunity to see my friends murderer sentenced. However, it is a very sad and somber occasion. Two boys are without their father's and I am without a very dear friend.

Mr. Foley, you fell prey to a woman who manipulated you to thinking my friend, Dr. John Yelenic, was evil and deserved to die. Nothing could be further from the truth.

John was a simple man who wanted a simple life. He wanted to be with his close friends, see his son grow up, practice dentistry in the town he and his family loved so much. He was generous to a fault and often helped those who were less fortunate. I saw that over and over again.

My most personal example is all he did to morally support me when I moved to California. My sister was pregnant and in her seventh month when my brother in law was given his deployment to Iraq. While everyone tried to tell me moving to California was a mistake, John was so supportive and understanding. He and I would talk every week sometimes for hours just laughing and joking. He would send my brother in law and his platoon care packages. He would call my sister and offer her his humor, prayers, support and love. No one in my family, especially my brother in law would forget that. When he returned from Iraq, he immediately sent John several of his decal's and awards because he knew how much John was proud of his country and supportive of his troops. John had them on his dresser until the day he died.

There was no reason for you to take him from us and especially in the manner that you chose to do it, so cruel and so cold blooded.

John's greatest joy and proudest accomplishment was being a Dad. You robbed him of that when you falsely accused him of horrible things and then manipulated Jay Jay into thinking his Daddy didn't love him anymore and didn't want to see him. Jay Jay wasn't even allowed to attend his funeral or say goodbye to his father. As a father yourself, you should have been more sympathetic to his plight. You should have worked hard to reunite him with his son instead of alienating him further.

I remember the day that John was going to be reunited with Jay Jay after 6 months of not seeing him and all the horrible things that ensued during that time, Lie Detector tests, interrogations and malicious accusations of unspeakable things. He was so excited to finally see Jay Jay and couldn't wait. He was going to give him the stuffed alligator we bought him on a trip to Las Vegas. It had a t-shirt on it that said "Crocodile Rock" because we got it at the Elton John concert. I will never forget the call I got that night, John, sobbing uncontrollably, telling me he lost his son forever. He told me that Jay Jay spit in his face and that you were screaming that he was a "molester" and that "he didn't love Jay Jay anymore" getting Jay Jay even more upset. John often referred to that day as the darkest he would ever know.

Even after that, John didn't lose his faith or his humor. He tried to believe in a system that didn't protect or help him. You were a part of that system Mr. Foley. You should have been objective. You shouldn't have let your temper get the best of you. You should have just let my friend live his life. He was ready to give up the majority of his estate to you and Michele, why couldn't that be enough?

I think back to the last conversation we had. (The Sunday before he was murdered) We talked for about 2 hours about the divorce being finalized, the party he was going to have (his 'freedom festival' entitled "Johnapalooza"), the "Sideways" wine tour trip we were going to take in Santa Barbara for my 29th birthday, and my brother in law getting ready for his second deployment to Iraq. When we hung up I can't remember if I told him I loved him. I usually did, but for some reason, I am drawing a blank on that conversation. I loved him. And I want him to know that I miss him terribly. I have learned that life is so much harder without a best friend. You go through life expecting death, expecting to lose the people you love, but you always think there will be someone (a best friend) to get you through it. Nothing has been harder in my life than losing him. I sank into a deep depression for the year after he was gone. I didn't sleep because of the nightmares I had of your heinous act, and the lack of progress on the case. I worked all the time and had little time for relationships. It wasn't until the summer after John's death when my father said to me "John would not approve of how you have been handling this" and I realized I needed help getting through this.

Its by the grace of God, John's other friends, Tim Abbey, Dennis Vaughn, Lisa Marple, Dave Lavrich, Debbie Jo Gresko, The Uss family, the McGuckin family, Mary Ann and Dave Clark, his Aunt Ruth, my own family and friends and especially my boyfriend, Mike that I was finally able to get through the dark time.

The hardest thing for me now is realizing Mike will never know John, our kids will never know him and that is a loss of such a huge magnitude to me. I wanted my husband and children to know John. I wanted him to be a part of our lives. And you robbed us of that opportunity.

When Jay Jay is old enough to know it, I will tell him about his Dad, how much he loved him and how Jay Jay was his proudest accomplishment. I will also tell him that my friendship with his Dad was one of the greatest joys of my life.

Mr. Foley, I pray your son forgives you someday for not being there to see him grow up, and help him cultivate his journey and all because you chose hate and you chose not to understand the plight of another father. Because you were selfish and chose to take our friend and brother away from us, I know I will never be able to forgive you, so I pray that he does.

Good morning. My name is Tim Abbey. I am a friend of John Yelenic's and I do not want to be here. How could any of us? But, I am not here to embrace his death, but to try and provide comfort to others through this time of grief and to celebrate John's life.

How do you sum up the life of someone whom to me was larger than life? I can not remember the exact moment I met John – some time in the early fall of 1985 on the 2nd floor of Sherwood Hall at Juniata College in Huntingdon. For the next 21 years, I knew a celebrity. Not in the sense that John was famous, but rather that he was a "personality". He was smart, opinionated, extremely funny, hopelessly talkative, loyal, kind, and generous beyond measure – always the life of the party.

Since last Thursday, I have tried to think of my favorite John moment – him wrapped in a silver suit running through Juniata dorms trying to soak people with his water guns, or the half wave/half salute he would throw out when entering a room or a party, or a dark night in the summer of 1988, after having a few too many beers, the two of us ended up being chased by some guys in Huntingdon, and while drunkenly running away through back yards, we flipped over a split-rail fence that we didn't see, or when he would clutch his chest like he was having a heart attack after a wild polka with my grandmother, or how him and Dennis would engage in intense, detailed discussions of not politics or social matters, but 1970's -1980's sitcoms, or maybe any number of stories not suitable for a House of God. But I don't have a favorite moment. John was more than just one moment in time – he was John - a constant source of laughter.

To Dave Lavrich and Dennis Vaughn, thank you for being there for John during the past few years. Without your friendship and support, I don't know how John would have survived. Because of the distance, my wife Heidi and I could not, and always felt like we were letting John down by not being there to support him. However, I am jealous of both of you though. Heidi and I were lucky if we saw John once a year. You saw him so many more times than I did since we all parted in 1989. You had so many more outrageous adventures.

John - it was an honor to have known you, to call you my friend, my brother. Save us good seats. We will catch up when we can. To the person or people who murdered him, I say, you can not comprehend what you have done. John may have lived alone and died alone, but he was never alone. John was loved by more people than you could have ever imagined. He was not just my friend. He was our friend. This will not stand.

Hi –Mary Ann Clark said to send this impact statement regarding the murder of Dr. John Yelenic to your attention. Please accept this statement on behalf of the entire John and Maribel Swasy family.

John Yelenic was a well-liked, highly-regarded dentist in his hometown of Blairsville.

But for the extended Swasy family, he will always be remembered as John John, the smiling little boy who used to play with his cousins out on the farm.

His mother, Mary Lois Swasy Yelenic, was forced to raise her son as a single mother, having lost her husband to a car crash when the baby was quite young.

Mary Lois worked hard as a school teacher to make sure young John John had a good home, surrounded with the love of her large, extended family. He excelled at school, and went on to college and dental school. While others left for the big city life, John returned to Blairsville so he could continue to be part of this warm family.

Sadly, he lost his mother to cancer, but he still had many aunts, uncles, cousins and scores of friends. And he had married Michele and they had adopted a baby they named Jay Jay. Like his mother, John worked very hard to provide for his family. But what many of us didn't realize was how tortured he was by Michele, who grew restless and tired of the marriage. Soon, it became evident as Michele used Jay Jay as a pawn to torment John, even having him arrested on false charges of child abuse.

After bailing on the marriage, Michele started dating Kevin Foley, a state trooper in Indiana. She shared her hatred of John, and grew even greedier, demanding more money, even though John paid her countless thousands of dollars for herself and their son.

Foley stoked the anger, as he played with knives and guns, he routinely talked of wanting John dead. Indeed, Foley tried to enlist other police officers to help him murder John. Just a few days before he committed murder, Foley even had the audacity to tell Barb Swasy, wife of John's cousin, Roger, that he wanted John dead.

Just before John was about to finalize his divorce and get on with his life, Foley completed his mission: Foley crept into John's home, then hacked poor John until he bled to death.

We weep that we couldn't save John from this horrific ordeal caused by Michele and Kevin Foley. We ache at the thought of John's final moments, his terror and struggle to save his life.

We thank God that John's fingernails provided the DNA to prove that Kevin Foley was the murderer. We hope justice will continue to be served, if others were involved in this heinous, pre-meditated hate crime.

We pray that Kevin Foley is punished for this senseless, brutal murder, which has left another Yelenic boy to grow up without a loving, sweet father.

Sarah R. Poje
Third Floor Courthouse
825 Philadelphia Street
Indiana, PA 15701

Kevin Foley Sentencing Statement

First of all, I'd like to take this opportunity to thank the court for allowing me to share the following impact statement with regard to the incomprehensibly depraved, unjustifiably horrific, and purely evil actions carried out by Kevin Foley on April 14th, 2006.

When John Yelenic was violently murdered by Mr. Foley, more than one life was viciously destroyed and ripped away from this world. Just like when a species dies out in nature, the impact of losing one life is far reaching and permanent. It has a ripple effect, and **life as we once knew it will never be the same.**

I do not personally know the countless details of pain, anger, rage, utter despair, and mind-altering dysphoria that John's family, friends, co-workers, neighbors, community, and other have felt for several years. But I know that in the wake of John's brutal death, his loss continues to **rip apart lives** and cause pain so deep and so numbing that it is also impossible to express. I only really know the details of how my life has been affected---John's murder has brought complete devastation to my family for the past three years.

Since John's death, Tim Abbey, my devoted husband of nearly 18 years and my best friend for 21 years has been tortured daily because of John's horrific death. In the fall of 2006, Tim uprooted his successful life in Connecticut and moved to Pennsylvania to be closer to the murder investigation, to have an impact on bringing John's murderers---**yes, murderers**---to justice. A man of the utmost integrity, loyalty, and justice, Tim sacrificed just about all of his own happiness, his own physical and mental well being, his career, and the psychological framework of his life to ensure that John's murderers would pay for this heinous crime. And he did it all for John, his friend, no---his "brother"---in this life. Tim did this all selflessly for John because that's the kind of guy that John was and that was the kind of friendship that they had. John wasn't a child molester as Michele brainwashed Mr. Foley to believe. John was everything but that. He loved with all of his heart. He was an amazing man, a true friend, someone who was really one of a kind. I had the honor of knowing John for most of my adult life and feel privileged to have called him my friend too. **This world is a darker place without him in it.**

I want Mr. Foley and everyone in the courtroom to know how my husband, Tim, spent countless hours on the phone and via email contacting and meeting with people all over Pennsylvania and across the U.S. to make sure that John's murder "would not stand." He devoted his time, his thoughts, and his energies to John's case, at the expense of so many other things including family, friends, and career. I know that many people who were more involved with this case than I have been would agree that, without Tim's and many other people's unending sacrifices, diligence, and convictions, Foley might not have been brought to justice today. The rage that my husband has experienced has nearly destroyed him. He is exhausted, numb, forever changed, and still so terribly sad because none of this can or ever will bring John back. All of this has taken a toll on many of the relationships Tim has and it may ultimately destroy our marriage, rendering my life irrevocably shattered, and the life of our 4-year-old son forever altered in a negative way. At least my son will still be able to grow up with a father though. You didn't give JJ that option; you ripped away his Daddy, his family, and his chances of ever having a normal life. How do you live with yourself, Mr. Foley? How could you do this? It is a question for which there will never be enough answers and a tragedy for which there will never, ever be enough healing or solace.

For you, Kevin Foley, I have nothing but utter disgust and contempt so black that it makes my head spin and my lungs choke. Your actions on April 14, 2006, did more than end John's precious life---it caused a series of events that rendered so many other lives shattered beyond repair. My only consolation is that I know John is looking down upon us now and offering up one of his famous, funny catch phrases, **"I can't be beat! I won't be beat!"** because you, Mr. Foley, are now going to pay for what you did. John's family and friends made sure of that and my husband, Tim, sacrificed everything to make sure of it.

So, Mr. Foley, as you go off to jail and face a heinous future of your own, perhaps the only redemption you may have left is to bring John's other murderers to light and to justice. The people who loved and still love John will not give up the fight, you can count on that.

Sincerely,

Heidi N. Abbey

Cc: Mary Ann Clark

The Honorable Judge William Martin,

It's hard for me to remember my life before April 13, 2006. I do recall being carefree, smiling easily and sleeping well.

My vocabulary never included gruesome words like murder, bludgeoned, exsanguinations or Kevin Foley.

I had never faced media phone calls and cameras.

That all changed that April day when Kevin Foley brutally murdered my cousin Dr. John Yelenic.

No more restful nights.

Laughter gave way to tears.

All because Kevin Foley, boyfriend of John's estranged wife, Michele, wanted him dead.

The afternoon when John's body was found at his house, I grieved for our loss. But I was consumed with guilt. You see, John new Kevin and Michele wanted him dead. Those of us closest to him heard only bits and pieces of his torment.

His murder began long before April 13, 2006. Michele made false charges of child abuse against John. John was handcuffed while seeing a patient taken to jail, subjected to lie detector tests and counseling. A vicious divorce, motivated by Michele's greed, made John's days and nights lonely as he was kept away from his beloved son Jay Jay. John was too embarrassed to tell all the details to family and friends.

Michele and Kevin wanted him dead, as she stood to get well over $1 million from his insurance and estate.

Yet with the help of dear friends, love and prayers, John was growing stronger. He told us he was about to sign the divorce papers. A light was at the end of this dark tunnel indeed, the last person to hear John speak of freedom was my mother, who planned on seeing him the next day.

Instead, we got phone calls from the coroner and Shoemaker Funeral Home. When they called Michele, still John's wife, as he was murdered hours before he signed the divorce papers, she brusquely said "do whatever you want" with John's body.

From that moment on, I vowed to myself, John and our family and friends, Kevin and Michele would be brought to justice.

My passion and determination grew. I was no longer naïve about State Police being here to protect us. One of their own, Kevin Foley, was lying and covering up this horrific crime.

My family and friends began to fear for my safety. As John's advocate, they worried that I could be the next of Foley's victims. I finally understood why John got out of town every weekend.

I was coached on watching where I parked my car and to check the rearview mirror. Some suggested that I get a gun. This was all so shocking to me. But I pushed on because I wasn't about to let John down.

You see, the John we all love was a picture of all things good. He always wanted to become a dentist and practice in his home town. He wanted a wife and family, which he thought he found with Michele and son Jay Jay. Instead, John's final days were marked with an empty heart and house, full of unopened gifts for the son Michele kept from him.

John was the most generous and loving man. He gave freely and would offer you the shirt off his back if he thought it would help.

He never knew hate, violence or greed. All of the vices that now find him dead.

In life John was a victim of the system. In death the system has set him free. Our hearts remain broken from the loss of this gentle soul.

Sincerely,

Mary Ann Clark

PENNSYLVANIA STATE TROOPERS ASSOCIATION
3625 Vartan Way, Harrisburg, Pa. 17110

FOR IMMEDIATE RELEASE
June 1, 2009

Contact: Bruce A. Edwards, President
800-541-9934

PSTA PRESIDENT ISSUES STATEMENT ON FOLEY SENTENCING

Indiana, Pa. – Pennsylvania State Troopers Association (PSTA) President Bruce A. Edwards today issued the following statement regarding the sentencing of Kevin Foley:

"Through the hard work and dedication of our Pennsylvania State Police, today a murderer will receive justice and face his sentencing in court. From the time the Blairsville Police asked the Pennsylvania State Police for assistance in this case, Cpls. Randy Gardner and Brian Zimmerman (from the Greensburg Station) worked tirelessly to solve this crime. They focused on the facts of the case and treated it like any other homicide. Today's sentencing is proof of their hard work and solid investigative skills. We should be grateful to them for ensuring that justice has been served.

"The PSTA also strongly supports and respects the men and women of the Troop A, Indiana Station. Like all troopers, they serve justice, no matter the outcome. Our dedicated state troopers from the Indiana Station continue to work to enforce the law, just as they have done for more than 100 years."

\# \# \#

About PSTA

PSTA represents 4,500 state police officers serving Pennsylvania. The Pennsylvania State Troopers Association exists to help protect those who protect us, and to serve those who serve the Commonwealth. For more information about PSTA, visit www.psta.org .

Kevin Foley was sentenced to a Murder of the First Degree, which by definition is a murder committed by an intentional killing. At the sentencing, Judge Martin stressed that Kevin Foley could have driven past Blairsville on his way home from the ice rink in Delmont to Indiana. He could have changed his mind at various points leading up to the entering of John Yelenic's home the evening of April 12, 2006. Why did Kevin Foley want to go to Blairsville? After all, it was out of his way. That question was never asked. Then again, Foley never admitted how his DNA got under John Yelenic's fingernails.

John Yelenic's murder did not fall within the guidelines of the 18 Aggravating Circumstances. Therefore, the death penalty was not sought by the state. However, the Yelenic case is classified as "on going."

PENNSYLVANIA CODE ON MURDER

18 Aggravating Circumstances

1. The victim was a firefighter, peace officer, public servant concerned in official detention, or assisting any law enforcement official in the performance of his duties, who was killed in the performance of his duties or as a result of his official position.

2. The defendant paid or was paid by another person or had contacted to pay or be paid by another person or had conspired to pay or be paid by another person for the killing of the victim.

3. The victim was being held by the defendant for ransom or reward, or as a shield or hostage.

4. The death of the victim occurred while defendant was engaged in the hijacking of an aircraft.

5. The victim was a prosecution witness to a murder or other felony committed by the defendant and was killed for the purpose of preventing his testimony against the defendant in any grand jury or criminal proceeding involving such offenses.

6. The defendant committed a killing while in the perpetration of a felony.

7. In the commission of the offense the defendant knowingly created a grave risk of death to another person in addition to the victim of the offense.

8. The offense was committed by means of torture.

9. The defendant has a significant history of felony convictions involving the use or threat of violence to the person.

10 The defendant has been convicted of another Federal or State offense, committed either before or at the time of the offense at issue, for which a sentence of life imprisonment or death was imposed or the defendant was undergoing a sentence of lie imprisonment for any reason at the time of the commission of the offense.

11. The defendant has been convicted of another murder committed in any jurisdiction and committed wither before or at the time of the offense at issue.

12. The defendant has been convicted of voluntary manslaughter, or a substantially equivalent crime in any other jurisdiction, committed either before at the time of the offense at issue.

13. The defendant committed the killing or was an accomplice in the killing, while in the perpetration of a felon under the provisions of the act of April 14, 1972 know as The controlled Substance,

Drug, Device and Cosmetic Act, and punishable under the provisions of drug trafficking sentencing and penalties.

14. At the time of the killing, the victim was or had been involved, associated or in competition with the defendant in the sale, manufacture, distribution or delivery f any controlled substance or counterfeit controlled substance in violation of The Controlled Substance, Drug, Device and Cosmetic Act or similar law of any other state, the District of Columbia or the United States, and the defendant committed the killing or was an accomplice to the killing as defined in 18 PA.C.S. *306 (c), and the killing resulted from or was related to that association, involvement or competition to promote the defendant's activities in selling, manufacturing, distributing or delivering controlled substances or counterfeit controlled substances.

15. At the time of the killing, the victim was or had been a nongovernmental informant or had otherwise provided any investigative law enforcement or police agency with information concerning criminal activity and the defendant committed the killing or was an accomplice to the killing, and the killing was in retaliation for the victim's activities as a nongovernmental informant or in providing information concerning criminal activity to an investigative, law enforcement or police agency.

16. The victim was a child under 12 years of age.

17. At the time of the killing, the victim as in her third trimester of pregnancy or the defendant had knowledge of the victim's pregnancy.

18. At the time of the killing the defendant was subjected to a court order restricting in any way the defendant's behavior toward the victim pursuant to (relating to protection from abuse) or any other order of a court of common pleas or of the minor judiciary designed in whole or in part of protect the victim from the defendant.

8. Mitigating Circumstances

1. The defendant has no significant history of prior criminal convictions.

2. The defendant was under the influence of extreme mental or emotional disturbance.

3. The capacity of the defendant to appreciate the criminality of his conduct or to conform his conduct to the requirements of the law as substantially impaired.

4. The age of the defendant at the time of the crime.

5. The defendant acted under extreme duress, although not such duress as to constitute a defense to prosecution under 18 Pa.C.S. *309 (relating to duress) or acted under substantial domination of another person.

6. The victim was a participant in the defendant's homicidal conduct or consented to the homicidal acts.

7. The defendant's participation in the homicidal act was relatively minor.

8. Any other evidence of mitigation concerning the character and record of the defendant and the circumstances of his offense.

GLOSSARY: TERMS PERTINENT TO THIS CASE

Arraignment:	Occurs three weeks after the preliminary hearing. This is when the defendant is told what he/she is charged with.
Appeal:	A request for an already decided case to be reviewed by a higher court.
Capital Case:	A case in which the death penalty is sought.
Civil Suit:	Brought forth by the victim's estate. This action must be filed within two years from the date of the victim's death. This suit can be brought against the defendants or third parties who caused the wrongful death of the victim.
Crime Report:	Once a crime has been reported, a police investigation begins.
Deoxyribonucleic Acid (DNA):	Is the genetic blueprint passed down from parent to child that encodes the human operating system.
Discovery:	The state is required to share all information it has collected in the case.
Felony:	A criminal offense punishable by imprisonment or death.
Motion:	A request made by an attorney that requires the judge to take some action.
Subpoena:	A court order which requires a witness to appear in court.
Preliminary Arraignment:	Shortly after the arrest the defendant is taken before a bail commissioner and asked if he/she has an attorney. If they do not, one will be appointed. In most murder cases, no bail is set at this time.
Preliminary Hearing:	Heard before a municipal judge. It is scheduled seven to ten days after the arrest.
Warrant:	A court order from a judge giving police authorization to search a particular place or arrest a certain person.

ABOUT THE AUTHOR

Andrea Niapas resides in Ligonier, Pennsylvania. She has degrees in education and sociology. As a documentarian she has researched and produced several films, focusing on popular women aviators of the "Golden Age" of aviation.

Recognizing that the death of an individual causes a ripple effect of pain and suffering among family members, friends, and community, she has become a victim's advocate, dedicating much of her time and resources to helping and giving a voice to the victims and co-victims of homicides.